THE LOST MUMMY OF DJEDHOR

sidestonepress

THE LOST MUMMY OF DJEDHOR

Reconstructing the burial of a Ptolemaic priest from Thebes

Maarten J. Raven

PALMA 33

PAPERS ON ARCHAEOLOGY OF THE LEIDEN MUSEUM OF ANTIQUITIES

PALMA: Papers on Archaeology of the Leiden Museum of Antiquities (volume 33)

Published by Sidestone Press, Leiden
www.sidestone.com
info@sidestone.nl
(+31)(0)71-7370131

Layout & cover design: Sidestone Press
Photographs cover: Robbert Jan Looman

ISBN 978-94-6426-344-2 (softcover)
ISBN 978-94-6426-345-9 (hardcover)
ISBN 978-94-6426-346-6(PDF e-book)

ISSN 2034-550X (print) | ISSN 2590-3012 (online)

DOI 10.59641/5v8020yh

Contents

Preface 7

PART I THE AUTOPSY AND ITS MUSEOLOGICAL CONTEXT 9

1. The Leiden mummy collection and its formation 11
2. Previous dissections 15
3. The acquisition of Djedhor's mummy 21
4. The 1878 autopsy 25
5. The *procès-verbal* 29

PART II DJEDHOR'S FUNERARY ENSEMBLE AND ITS PARALLELS 41

6. Numbering issues 43
7. The cartonnage 45
8. The garlands 51
9. The bead net 55
10. Outer wrappings 57
11. Anklets and sandals 61
12. The Book of the Dead papyrus 65
13. Amuletic necklace 69
14. Inner wrappings 71
15. Mummification techniques 87
16. Other burial gifts 89

PART III DJEDHOR'S BURIAL AND ITS ARCHAEOLOGICAL CONTEXT 99

17. Date 101
18. Social status 103
19. Provenance 107
20. Conclusion 111

Appendix 1: Comments by Leemans 113
Appendix 2: Reply by Pleyte 117
List of illustrations 119
Abbreviations 121
Bibliography 123
Index 127

Preface

In a hidden corner of the rich archives of the Leiden Museum of Antiquities lies a fascinating manuscript dealing with the autopsy on an Ancient Egyptian mummy. This was performed in 1878 by the Museum's curator Willem Pleyte, a well-known Egyptologist and meticulous researcher who had done some similar interventions on Pharaonic Period mummies before. Like these previous specimens, the mummy dissected in 1878 was rapidly disintegrating in the Dutch climate. Thanks to Pleyte's detailed *procès-verbal*, the mummy (which had to be discarded soon after the autopsy and is thereby lost for further research) can be reconstructed at least on paper, which allows us to recognize it as the remains of an elite burial in Ptolemaic Thebes. The dilapidated remains of the mummy's cartonnage, together with various items of funerary jewellery, decorated textiles, and inscribed material on linen and papyrus retrieved by Pleyte from the mummy wrappings – all still kept in the Leiden collections – help us to date the burial and identify its owner as a priest called Djedhor. Moreover, several comparable funerary items in other museums in Europe, Egypt and the United States allow us to visualise the additional funerary material once present in the tomb, such as the mummy's coffins, canopic chest, stela, and Ptah-Sokar-Osiris statue. Finally, the common acquisition history of all these items enables us to make a guess concerning the original location of Djedhor's tomb and to suggest through whose hands his remains passed on his way to Leiden.

The present study was originally conceived as a chapter for a new book on mummy research recently performed on the rich collections of the Leiden Museum. This would have included reports on various modern scientific investigations of Ancient Egyptian human and animal remains, as well as some highlights of previous analyses executed on this material in the course of the two centuries of the Museum's existence. For various reasons, this publication could not be realised in the format originally foreseen. It was felt, however, that the following study (which had already been finished) deserves to be published in full, especially since the archival material on which it is based has already been quoted several times in previous publications on the Leiden mummy collection or the Museum's history. For the present publication, an introductory section was added with an outline of the genesis of the Leiden mummy collection, the early research on this material, and the acquisition of the Djedhor mummy ensemble. Most of these data were published before, but sometimes only in Dutch, so the present occasion was used to present this material in an English translation. The rest of the text was extended with some more details and extra photographs. At the end, two further relevant manuscripts from the RMO archives have been included as well.

I am very grateful for the opportunity offered by the editors of PALMA for inclusion of this interesting autopsy and its aftermath in the present series, and to Sidestone Press for their pleasant cooperation and great care. Special thanks are due to Mariëlle Bulsink for help in the RMO library and archives, to Sofia Häggman (Stockholm) and Ms M. Heckhoff (Leipzig) for information on the relevant material in the collections for which they care, to John Taylor and Tamás Mekis for further references to parallels, and to Koen Donker van Heel, Petra Hogenboom and Sven Vleeming for checking some inscriptions. Most illustrations were prepared by the Museum's photographer Robbert Jan Looman, whom I thank for his meticulous work and excellent assistance.

PART I

THE AUTOPSY AND ITS MUSEOLOGICAL CONTEXT

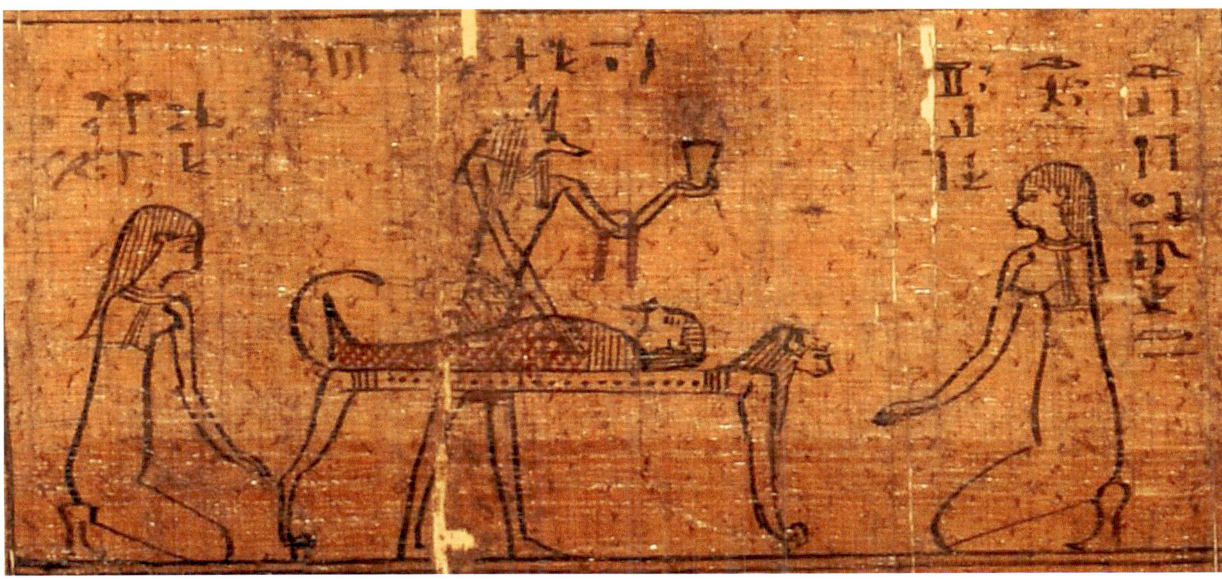

Fig. 1. Anubis embalming Djechor's body. Detail of Djedhor's Book of the Dead papyrus (RMO, inv. AL 61 vel 15).

Fig. 2. Caspar Reuvens, the first director of the Leiden Museum (1818–1835). Undated portrait by Louis Moritz (Collection Leiden University).

Chapter 1

The Leiden mummy collection and its formation

1.1. The Leiden Museum of Antiquities

The National Museum of Antiquities in Leiden, the Netherlands (*Rijksmuseum van Oudheden*, henceforth abbreviated as RMO), was founded in 1818 and holds archaeological collections from Egypt, the Ancient Near East, the classical world (Greeks, Romans and Etruscans), and the Netherlands.[1] Its foundation dates to the period immediately after the Napoleonic era, when the Netherlands had rather unexpectedly become an independent monarchy for the first time in its existence, and when the newly appointed King William I was looking for initiatives to manifest his country's political and cultural ambitions within the European context. It was the explicit task of the Museum's first director, Caspar Reuvens (1793–1835, Fig. 2), to create a national archaeological collection which would be able to compete with similar European institutions such as the British Museum or the Louvre. As a result of Napoleon's Egyptian expedition (1798–1801), the mysterious heritage of the Pharaohs occupied a central position both in contemporary academic research and in the interest of the cultural elite. Accordingly, Ancient Egyptian remains ranged very high on the wishlist of the newly created museum. Thanks to Reuvens's active acquisition policy, the Leiden Museum soon ranged among the most important Egyptian collections in the world.[2] Today, with about 22.500 Egyptian objects in total, it is certainly not one of the largest collections of its kind, but of course it is not quantity but quality which counts, and therefore the Leiden Egyptian department can be reckoned among the ten best collections worldwide. Certain categories of objects are very well represented, and among these is the collection of mummies. This consists of no less than 31 human mummies, 30 mummy parts (such as heads, hands, or braids of hair), and 69 animal mummies (mammals, birds, reptiles, and fish).

1.2. Early acquisitions of mummies

A complete catalogue of the mummy collection has been published in 2005.[3] This publication already includes a chapter providing information on the acquisition of the various items, their previous owners, and their original provenance.[4] Obviously, it will be impossible to repeat all the documentation gathered there, but I shall concentrate here on some

1 For an overview of the museum's history, edited on the occasion of its bicentennial, see Ter Keurs/Wirtz 2018.

2 For Reuvens, see M. Hoijtink, in: Ter Keurs/Wirtz 2018, 43–50; cf. Bierbrier 2019, 390.

3 Raven/Taconis 2005. Please note that one more human head and one bird mummy have been acquired since this publication came out (see *infra*, n. 27).

4 *Ibid.*, 19–33.

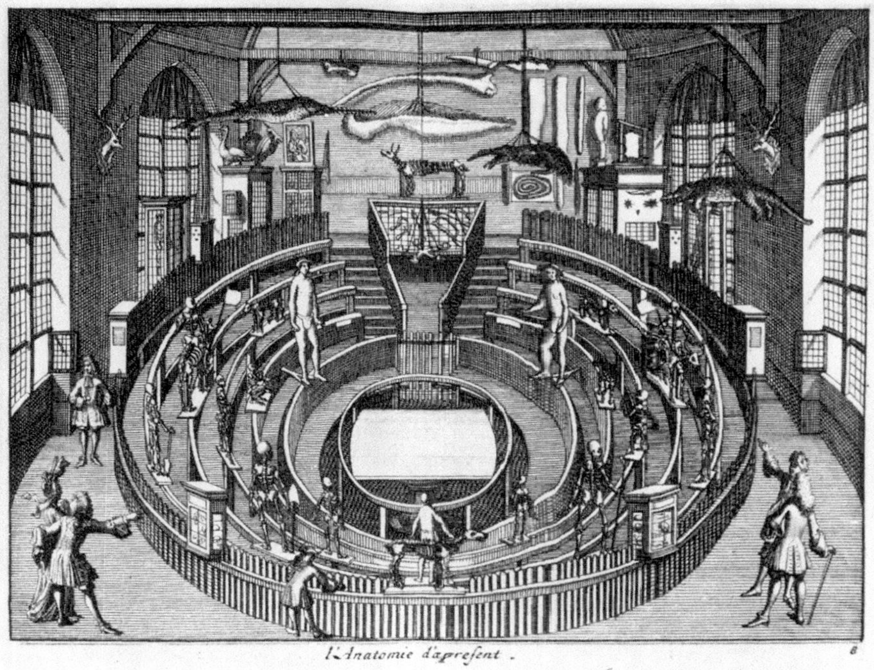

Fig. 3. The Theatrum Anatomicum in 1712. Wellcome Library (inv. no. 20254i).

episodes which may help to understand the circumstances of the acquisition of Djedhor's mummy.[5] For the first mummies to reach Leiden we have to go back to the early seventeenth century. The foundation of Leiden University in 1575 stimulated an interest in medical studies, and in 1593 a *Theatrum Anatomicum* or lecture theatre for performing dissections was installed. This included a display of skeletons and anatomical samples, and from 1620 also a number of Egyptian mummies or their parts (Fig. 3). What remained of these items was donated to the RMO in 1821, followed by a second lot in 1872.[6]

By the time these items arrived in the RMO, they were hardly in a presentable condition, having suffered from two centuries of neglect and poor climatic circumstances in the damp church housing the *Theatrum*. This presented a problem, because Reuvens was well aware of the importance of this kind of funerary material for a representative display of Ancient Egyptian culture. Moreover, he had a strong personal interest in this aspect of pharaonic material heritage. Therefore, in 1824 he purchased a mummy which had arrived in Ghent (now in Belgium, but then still part of the Netherlands) on board of one of the ships of the Flemish merchant Jean-Baptiste De Lescluze (1780–1858, see Fig. 8).[7] The mummy was lying in a painted coffin, which also contained a cat mummy – doubtless added by the art dealers to make the sale more attractive (Fig. 6). The ensemble had already been on display in Bruges and Ghent for several weeks before Reuvens managed to acquire it for the RMO. However, upon arrival in Leiden Reuvens decided to investigate the mummy, and before the invention of radiography there was only a single method to do so: the highly destructive practice of dissection. Accordingly, he invited the Ghent professor of natural history, J.G.S. van Breda (who had already applied for permission to investigate the mummy when it was still in Belgium), as well as the Leiden anatomist G. Sandifort. On 7 June, 1824, the three scholars opened both the human mummy and the one of the cat – and by the time they had finished their autopsy, Reuvens was again left without a suitable mummy to show to the visitors of his museum.

Having made the acquantaince of De Lescluze, one of the first merchants to resume the Mediterranean trade after the Napoleonic wars, Reuvens decided to employ this useful contact for the acquisition of further Egyptian collections. Already in July 1824 he sent De Lescluze a list of suggestions, which mentioned in the first place: *well-*

5 See also Chapter 3 below.

6 For the *Theatrum Anatomicum*, see Raven 1993, 23–27; Raven/Taconis 2005, 19–20, 324 (inv.nos. Ar 34, Ar 36a,c), 325 (inv. nos. Ar 32a, Ar 34c–d, Ar 35–36, Ar 36b); Raven, in: Ter Keurs/Wirtz 2018, 17–22.

7 For this episode, see Raven 1993, 34–38; Raven/Taconis 2005, 21–22, 324 (inv.no. L 1), 328 (inv.no. L 2); Raven, in: Ter Keurs/Wirtz 2018, 67–68. For De Lescluze, see Bierbrier 2019, 278.

preserved mummies which have not been opened.[8] Although the letter in question did not reach the Flemish merchant on time, De Lescluze had already bought some relevant material upon his own initiative, so that there were indeed three mummies present in the Antwerp auction organized by him on 5 July, 1826. These were instantly bought there by Reuvens, together with over eighty other highlights of the sale.[9] One of these mummies was the specimen which forms the subject of the present study and which can now be properly identified as that of the Theban priest Djedhor.

The same year saw the arrival of a set consisting of a mummy and three coffins, belonging to another Theban priest by the name of Ankhhor.[10] This was acquired from the Flemish colonel B.E.A. Rottiers (1771–1858) who had been sent out to the Greek archipelago, charged with a special mission for the acquisition of antiquities for the RMO. Though the Egyptian burial in question had allegedly been found in Famagusta on Cyprus, it is more probable that Rottiers bought the objects in Smyrna, where he resided between his various trips to the Greek isles and where Egyptian antiquities were imported on a regular basis at the time.

Another person who functioned as an agent for the Leiden Museum was the Dutch painter Jean-Emile Humbert (1771–1839), one of the discoverers of ancient Carthage and later stationed at Leghorn.[11] This Italian town was not only closely situated to Tuscany and its fabulous Etruscan collections, it was also the harbour where shiploads of Egyptian antiquities used to arrive at irregular intervals and where several other European museums kept their lookouts (inclusing no less than Jean-François Champollion, working for the Louvre). Humbert's first success in 1827 was the acquisition of the Egyptian collection of Maria Cimba (the widow of Dr Cimba, Henry Salt's personal physician, who had picked up hundreds of pharaonic objects in the wake of his master, the famous British consul-general in Alexandria).[12] These included some heads and hands of human mummies (which have been lost in the meantime), plus ten animal mummies which are still part of the Leiden collections. More important was Humbert's purchase of the first collection of Giovanni d'Anastasi, consul-general for Norway and Sweden in Alexandria, in 1828.[13] The sale's catalogue included almost 6,000 objects, among which were 27 human and 40 animal mummies. This acquisition immediately made the Leiden collection of mummies one of the largest in the world. Eleven of these mummies were lying in a single coffin, seven in a double one, two had three, and one even four coffins. All this ensures that we possess a good documentation on the identity of these human remains, and in most cases know their date and provenance.

1.3. Mummy acquisitions after Reuvens

After the death of Reuvens in 1835, the days of the great acquisitions were over. All the same, some more mummies could be added by his successor, Conrad Leemans (1809–1893, Fig. 4).[14] Thus in 1846, the French physician Antoine Clot-Bey donated eleven animal mummies,[15] and four more were purchased from the estate of N.H. van Beeftingh, a Dutchman who had spent some time in Egypt.[16] In 1886, two mummies and coffins from Maspero's excavations at Akhmim were bought via J.H. Insinger and V. de Stuers.[17]

Leemans finally retired as museum director in 1891. He was succeeded by the Egyptologist Willem Pleyte (1836–1903, Fig. 5), who had shown a vivid interest in mummies while still a curator (from 1869 onwards).[18] Even so, this was not reflected in his acquisition policy, since only two mummy heads and one hand were added to the collections during his period of office.[19] After his death in 1903 the direction of the museum passed into the hands of non-Egyptologists, and the slow increase of the mummy collection continued, with just one more head and a single falcon mummy.[20] This changed once again for a more rapid growth when a succession of three Egyptologists took over from 1939 onwards.[21] Still, the mummy collection mainly profited from donations. Two mummy heads, one

---

8 Archives RMO, Letters dispatched 22 July 1824; see now https://www.archieven.rmo.nl/wp-content/object_files/003.pdf#page=369–370. Quoted in Raven/Taconis 2005, 22.

9 For this acquisition, see Raven/Taconis 2005, 22–23, 324 (inv.nos. L.XII.1–3: 3 human mummies), 328 (inv.nos. L.XII.4–7: 4 animal mummies); Raven, in: Ter Keurs/Wirtz 2018, 67–71. See also below, § 3.1, were more details are given about this important sale.

10 See Raven 1993, 43–47; Raven/Taconis 2005, 23–25, 324 (inv. no. RO.III).

11 For Humbert, see Halbertsma 2003, 71–111; R.B. Halbertsma, in: Ter Keurs/Wirtz 2018, 94–99, 103–113.

12 For this collection, see L. Weiss and I. Morfini, in: Ter Keurs/Wirtz 2018, 86–92. Cf. Raven 1993, 48; Raven/Taconis 2005, 25, 327 (inv.nos. CI 254, 256, 259–260, 281, 335).

13 For the Anastasi sale, see Raven 1993, 48–49; Halbertsma 2003, 99–107; Raven/Taconis 2005, 26–27, 324 (inv.nos. AMM 1–27c), 325 (inv.nos. AMM 13c–27d), 327 (inv.nos. AMM 13b–16s); Raven, in: Ter Keurs/Wirtz 2018, 72–78; R.B. Halbertsma, in: Ter Keurs/Wirtz 2018, 108–113. For Anastasi as a person, see V. Verschoor, in: Ter Keurs/Wirtz 2018, 79–85.

14 For Leemans, see Bierbrier 2019, 270–271.

15 Raven/Taconis 2005, 327 (inv.nos. CB 1–11).

16 *Ibid.*, 327 (inv.nos. BA 216c–d, 217–218).

17 For these acquisitions, see Raven/Taconis 2005, 28, 324 (inv.nos. AdS 1 and AES 14); Raven 2018, 29–31, 59, 63–64 with fig. II.17.

18 For Pleyte, see Bierbrier 2019, 371; Raven, in: Ter Keurs/Wirtz 2018, 169–173. See also below, § 2.2.

19 See Raven/Taconis 2005, 325 (inv.nos. F 93/1.22, F 96/5.1, and F 1902/5.10).

20 *Ibid.*, 325 (inv.no. F 1910/5.1), 327 (inv.no. F 1910/5.2).

21 W.D. van Wijngaarden (director from 1939–1957), A. Klasens (1957–1978), and H.D. Schneider (1978–1988).

Fig. 4. Conrad Leemans, the second director of the Leiden Museum (1839–1891). Undated photograph (Archives RMO).

Fig. 5. Willem Pleyte, the third director of the Leiden Museum (1891–1903). Undated photograph (Archives RMO).

hand, and four animal mummies were donated by the heirs of J.H. Insinger in 1956,[22] and in 1975 the museum received a private donation consisting of eight falcon mummies.[23] Other donations dating to the same decennia included four mummy heads, a hand, an ibis, two falcons, and a crocodile.[24] One hand and one ibis mummy were purchased,[25] plus two child mummies dating to the Roman Period.[26] Finally, in recent years two more donations were acquired: a mummy head and a falcon mummy.[27]

---

22 Raven/Taconis 2005, 326 (inv.nos. F 1956/10.1–3) and 327–328 (inv. nos. F 1956/10.4–7); Raven 2018, 47 with figs. II.50–53.

23 Raven/Taconis 2005, 328 (inv.nos. F 1982/12.7–14).

24 *Ibid.*, 325–327 (inv.nos. F 1942/6.1, F 1960/1.1, F 1973/9.53, F 1986/3.1, F 1975/11.3–4, F 1998/11.2–3).

25 *Ibid.*, 326 (inv.no. F 1948/12.2), 327 (F 1954/11.2).

26 *Ibid.*, 324 (inv.nos. F 1980/1.12 and F 1985/3.1).

27 Inv.nos. F 2004/12.2 and F 2010/8.2, respectively. For more information on these objects (and on all other RMO inventory numbers mentioned in the present book), see https://www.rmo.nl/en/collection/search-collection/.

Chapter 2

Previous dissections

2.1. The 1824 autopsy by Reuvens

In 1895, Wilhelm Conrad Röntgen published an account of his discovery of a new type of electromagnetic radiation which in many languages is still referred to by his name. One year later, experiments by his assistant Walter König pointed out that the new 'X-rays' were highly suitable for the investigation of (among others) Egyptian mummies. This revolution thereby provided a welcome alternative for the tool so far used for mummy research: the scalpel or dissection knife.[28] The human mummies in Leiden were first radiographed by P.H.K. Gray in 1965.[29] Before that, all analyses performed on the Leiden mummies were done in a destructive manner, by unwrapping and dissection.

In other countries, the first instances of such unwrappings have been recorded for the 17th and 18th centuries, with public sceances by, among others, Hadley (1763) or Blumenbach (1790).[30] For the Netherlands, the first autopsy took place in 1771, albeit on a mummy which has proved to be a fake in the light of modern research.[31] The earliest known event within the walls of the RMO has already been mentioned above, and consisted of the autopsy of the Ghent mummy acquired in 1824.[32] Less than one month after its arrival at the RMO, on June 7th, Reuvens and his two colleagues Van Breda and Sandifort opened the linen wrappings of the human mummy (so far believed to be that of an Egyptian princess) and of the cat accompanying her inside the coffin (Fig. 6). A vivid report of their intervention was duely published on August 27:[33]

> *All bystanders were covered by the fine powder that rose from the wrappings at the least disturbance. The wrappings consisted of cotton*[34] *of various ranges of texture; those closest to the body, which therefore were not visible before the uppermost ones had been unwrapped, consisted of a very coarse weave; both arms had first been wrapped in a separate bandage, then united with the torso by means of two bandages starting at each hand, then after having served to wrap the hands continuing upwards over the arms, passing around the neck, crossing over the chest, and knotted together on the back; the above-mentioned fine powder was found between some layers of these wrappings, and especially in the cavities of abdomen and thorax* [...] *Within the bandages and embedded in the powder lay the skeleton of a young adult woman, completely intact except for a few bones of the toes; some remains of sinews or muscles were only visible at the tibia and*

28 Cf. Raven/Taconis 2005, 42ff.
29 Gray 1966; cf. Raven/Taconis 2005, 44 with figs. II.3a–d.
30 Raven 1993, 32; Raven/Taconis 2005, 41–42.
31 Raven 1984–1985; Raven 1993, 32; Raven/Taconis 2005, 42.
32 *Supra*, § 1.2.
33 Reuvens/Sandifort/Van Breda 1824, partly quoted in Raven 1993, 37 (in Dutch, here translated into English).
34 *Sic!* Of course, in fact the wrappings were made of linen. This has been confirmed by modern research of the wrappings still remaining in the RMO; see Van 't Hooft *et al.* 1994, 2–3, 70–72 (cat.nos. 114–124).

Fig. 6. The Ghent mummy in its coffin, also containing a cat mummy. Lithograph by Kierdorff (Archives RMO).

fibula; no muscles of any other parts of the body could be found, nor remains of the internal organs of abdomen or thorax; no trace could be detected of the hair or the nails; and the bandages around the pelvic bones and elsewhere had been applied in such a manner that it became obvious that the body had only been wrapped after the removal of the internal organs and the muscles. The pelvis was completely empty, but the nose had not been broken, and accordingly the brain was not removed from the skull via that route, which Herodotus asserts that was sometimes done.[35]

The mummy of a young cat was present in the same coffin used for the human mummy. Inside was the animal, complete with skin and fur; the rear legs had been placed against the torso, with the front legs in between; a single sheet of cotton had been rolled around the cat, stuck on the animal by a bituminous substance, though so thin that the fur had not clotted together, perhaps this was the substance which Herodotus calls kommi. Around this sheet were some cotton bandages, the inner ones more coarse and being fixed around the cat by means of a length of two-ply string; the bandages around the head painted on the outside with a cat figure, and the ears added in pieces of cloth, because the real ears had been covered by the wrappings.

The powder found during the autopsy was demonstrated to be calcium carbonate during a later analysis by the chemist Eyben.[36] It had originally been contained in some kind of bag inside the wrappings: a highly unusual mummification technique which had not been very effective for the preservation of the female body in question. Thus, this event of 7 June, 1824, was not very instructive and did not produce any of the small burial gifts so often present within the mummy wrappings. Moreover, the dissection proved to be so fatal for the preservation of the mummy that once again Reuvens had nothing to show the visitors of his museum. The skeleton survived and was subsequently given to the Anatomical Museum of Leiden University (where it cannot be identified nowadays), whereas the remains of the wrappings and of the cat are still kept in one of the storerooms of the RMO. Therefore, the outcome of this dissection was that Reuvens soon formulated his conviction as follows:[37]

In general one should preserve mummies intact, because once opened they will be lost. One can obtain a better impression of the concrete object as long as the principal element and its accessories are still united and in their pristine state, rather than when its various components have become separated and their lack of mutual connection has to be compensated by a written explanation which one cannot visualise. As regards the need to become acquainted with the various components which make up the total of a mummy and its appurtenances, Messrs. excavators and the Arabs take good care to smash a sufficient number of mummies for supplying our museums copiously with all sorts of minor objects which are to be found inside their wrappings.

2.2. Dissections of the later 19th century

On the whole, this sound principle was respected by the Leiden Museum during the following decennia, when the mummy collection witnessed a spectacular growth. Even so, a limited number of autopsies was executed on certain items which had started deteriorating in the damp climate inside the inadequate museum building of the time, which suffered of a leaking roof, a broken-down sewer system, and the impossibility to heat the galleries due to the absence of chimneys. As a result of this, a number of mummies had to be discarded because of decay, and dissection formed the last opportunity to investigate their contents before they were de-accessioned. Thus, on October 17, 1839, a cat mummy was unwrapped which so far had still been contained in a rectangular coffin inscribed with a formula for the goddess Bastet; even so, Leemans described this item as the mummy of a hare in his catalogue of the Egyptian collection.[38]

More dissections took place when Willem Pleyte joined the staff of the museum in 1869. Thus in 1872 he performed a number of autopsies on several badly deteriorated mummies discovered in the same year on an attic of the Leiden University library. Clearly, these were the forgotten remains of the Egyptian material originally shown in the *Theatrum Anatomicum*, part of which had already been presented to the RMO in 1821.[39] Pleyte soon found out that the larger mummy, which had formed a highlight of the 17th-century display (Fig. 3, showcase in right-hand corner at the rear, with the coffin displayed on top), consisted of the wrapped body of an adult woman. Ages of decay, together with the detrimental effect of bituminous substances, had utterly destroyed the skeleton and other

35 Obviously this refers to Herodotus' famous description in his *Histories*, Book II, 85ff.

36 Raven 1993, 38.

37 Reuvens 1830, 44–45 note *c*; quoted in Raven 1993, 39; Raven/Taconis 2005, 22.

38 Leemans 1840, 196, no. N 16. For this episode, see Raven 1993, 55–56 with fig. 80; Raven/Taconis 2005, 28.

39 Cf. *supra*, n. 6.

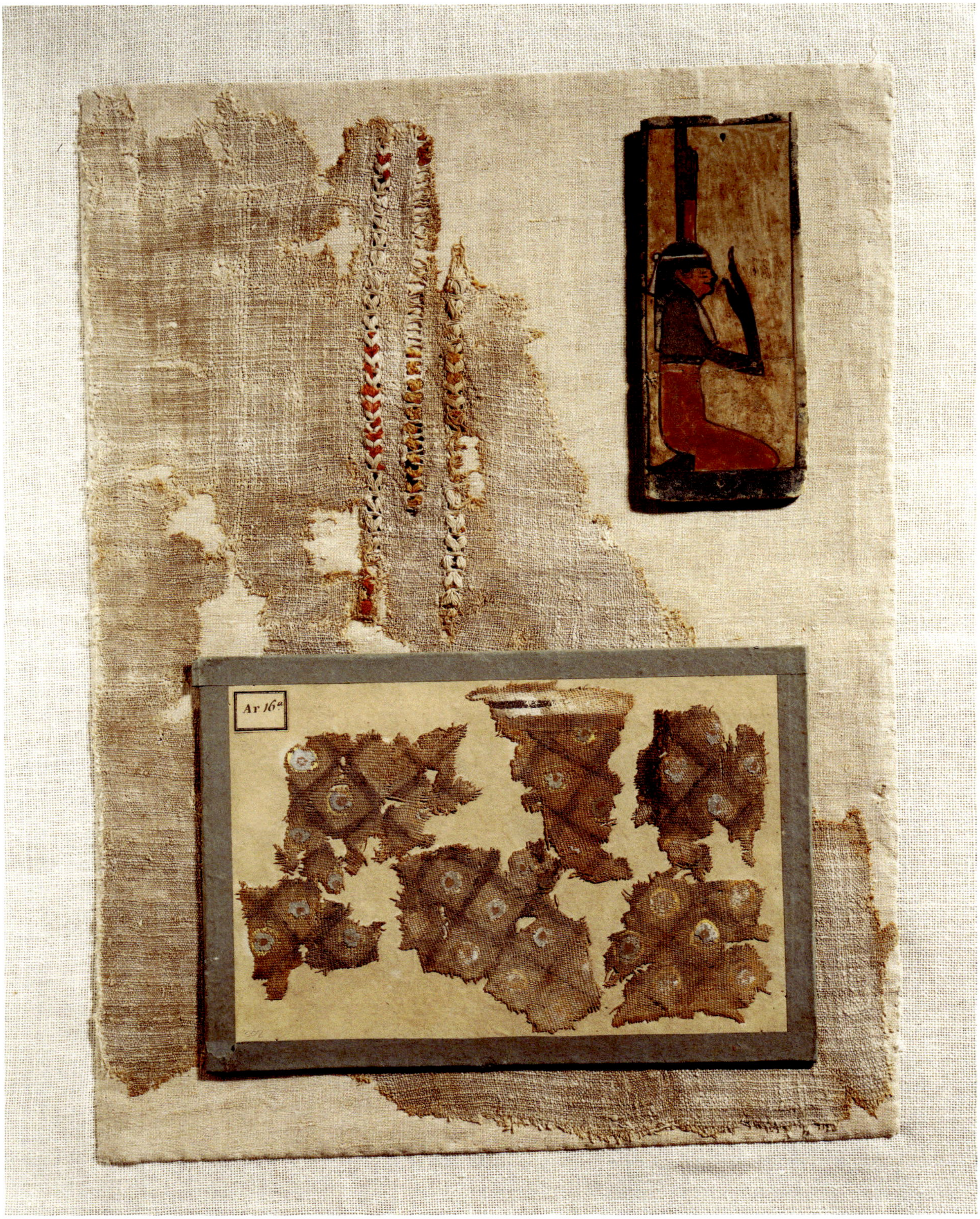

Fig. 7. Remains of the painted and embroidered bandages of the large mummy, plus a cartonnage panel taken from the third mummy (RMO, inv. Ar32b and Ar 34a).

tissues, so that only the skull and some samples of textile could be preserved (Fig. 7).[40]

A smaller specimen, which during its stay in the *Theatrum Anatomicum* had always been regarded as the mummy of an Egyptian princess due to its rich apparel of a mask, five cartonnage collars, and a ditto foot-cover, proved to consist of a modern fake: the legs of an adult had been joined to a child mummy by fixing the two parts between two planks, which were then wrapped with modern rope and a number of ancient textiles. The child mummy is incomplete and utterly disjointed, suggesting it was already in decay when it was wrapped.[41]

During the same occasion, Pleyte investigated a third mummy from the original *Theatrum Anatomicum*, which had already been transferred to the RMO in 1821. This proved to be the remains of an adult man, once again badly corroded by the application of excessive amounts of oils or resins. Pleyte could do no more than describe the disposition of the remaining bandages, though he also kept the legs and a small panel of cartonnage for the collection (Fig. 7).[42]

Although the outcome of these dissections was in fact rather disappointing, a detailed *procès-verbal* of each of them can be found in the Museum's archives.[43] This clearly shows Pleyte as a meticulous observer who was well aware of his responsabilities, as the last person to record the peculiarities of these items before their de-accessioning from the collections. At the same time, these autopsies can be regarded as preliminaries to the much more rewarding dissection of Djedhor's mummy which took place in 1878 and forms the main subject of the present publication.[44]

Another autopsy was performed by a certain Dr W.K.J. Schoor on one of the cat mummies donated by Clot-Bey.[45] This was carried out in July 1891, the very month of Pleyte's appointment as the Museum's new director. The report gives some details of the textiles used for the wrappings, describes the orange-brown fur of the animal, and notes that the bones are heavier than those of a modern domestic cat.[46]

A final instance of such a destructive procedure was the dissection of the decaying mummy of Djedmonthefankh in 1892. This had been acquired from Anastasi in 1829, lying in one of the most beautiful coffins of the collection (inv.no. AMM 18). The autopsy was performed by the Museum's amanuensis and produced perfect dating evidence in the shape of two leather braces stamped with the name of Osorkon I (924–909 BC). Under the shroud fixed by means of five transverse straps the mummy proved to be in a sorry state of decomposition, so that most of its remains could not be preserved.[47] This appears to have been the last dissection performed within the walls of the RMO. Three years later Roentgen's discovery provided an alternative and non-destructive method to analyse mummies, whereas the move of the RMO to new premises around 1920 put an end to the constant deterioration of this vulnerable material. Therefore, the remaining mummies could be preserved intact and still form a precious collection for the enjoyment of the museum visitors and the benefit of scientific research.

In view of the present-day discussions about the ethics of handling and displaying human remains it may be useful to add that no mummies (whether human of animal) were dissected within the walls of the Leiden Museum, unless it proved to be impossible to preserve them and they started forming a risk for contamination of the rest of the collection or a danger to the health of the museum employees and visitors. No dissections were ever performed for the mere entertainment of spectators or in the presence of onlookers. According to an unconfirmed tradition among the museum staff, the remaining skeletal material and human tissue was properly interred on one of the Leiden cemeteries, probably the main general cemetery situated along the Groenesteeg. However, in spite of recent queries (2024) this story could not be confirmed by the cemeteries in question.

40 Raven 1993, 57–59 with fig. 84; Raven/Taconis 2005, 28–29, 211 cat. 35 (inv.no. Ar 34c). For the wrappings, see Van 't Hooft *et al.* 1994, 4, 92 (cat.no. 195).

41 Raven 1993, 58–59 with fig. 83; Raven/Taconis 2005, 29 and 165, cat. 22 (inv.no. Ar 36a,c). For the wrappings, see Van 't Hooft *et al.* 1994, 4, 95–96, 192 (cat.nos. 208–209, 475).

42 Raven 1993, 59 with fig. 84; Raven/Taconis 2005, 29. The legs were discarded at a later stage.

43 Archives RMO, 6.4.3/3 *sub* 2.1.

44 *Infra*, Chapters 4–5.

45 *Supra*, n. 15. For the wrappings, see Van 't Hooft *et al.* 1994, 4, 89 (cat.no. 183).

46 Raven 1993, 74 with fig. 106; Raven/Taconis 2005, 31. See RMO Archives, 6.4.3/3 *sub* 2.2, inv.no. CB 3; drawings 23.3/2.21-22.

47 Raven 1993, 74–75; Raven/Taconis 2005, 30; RMO Archives, 6.4.3/3 *sub* 2.1 (inv.no. AMM 18), drawings 23.3/3.14. For the wrappings, see Van 't Hooft *et al.* 1994, 4, 73–74 (cat.nos. 125–128).

Fig. 8. Portrait of Jean-Baptiste de Lescluze (private collection, Belgium).

Chapter 3

The acquisition of Djedhor's mummy

3.1. An unfortunate auction

Above, reference was already made to the Flemish merchant Jean-Baptiste De Lescluze (1780–1858, Fig. 8).[48] He was one of the first merchants to resume the Dutch commerce with the Mediterranean countries after the end of the Napoleonic wars. Thus, as early as 1821, he already sent two ships to the Greek archipelago, a mission that had the bad luck to coincide with a revolt against the Turkish oppression and therefore was not crowned by success. A second expedition in 1822–1823 visited the Black Sea and also passed by Alexandria. On February 1, 1824, one of De Lescluze's ships returned to Bruges from Smyrna, carrying the mummy which was so successfully exhibited in Bruges and Ghent and which was later dissected by Reuvens.[49] At that moment, De Lescluze himself was already back in Egypt where in April 1824 he bought a collection of antiquities from François Barthou, a well-known dealer who also directed excavations on behalf of others.[50] This cargo was shipped to Antwerp in 1825, where Reuvens inspected it at the beginning of March 1825 – incognito, in order not to raise financial expectations. At the same moment, De Lescluze's wife had already started negotiations about the sale of the collection to the Ministry of Education. These did not produce any results before De Lescluze himself returned from the Orient in February 1826, rather embittered because his commercial adventures had led to legal and financial complications in Alexandria and his enterprise was threatened by bankruptcy.

There seemed to be only one solution: to have the collection of *Aegyptiaca* auctioned as soon as possible to prevent further trouble. However, again De Lesluze had bad luck, because after the sale had been fixed to take place in Antwerp on July 5, 1826, the printed catalogue was delayed and did not find distribution among prospective buyers.[51] Accordingly, Reuvens turned out to be the only bidder at the auction and managed to acquire all the most important items, such as three rolls of papyrus, three mummies,[52] several stelae, the best of the alabaster vases, a large stone sarcophagus, and numerous

48 See n. 7. For De Lescluze, see also Van de Walle 1959–1960; Raven, in: Ter Keurs/Wirtz 2018, 67–68; Bierbrier 2019, 278.

49 See *supra*, § 2.1.

50 For Barthou or Barthow, see Bierbrier 2019, 38.

51 For the catalogue, see Anonymous 1826.

52 In his *Aanmerkingen* (below, Appendix 1, page 1 n. *a*) Leemans erroneously states that the three mummies were not bought at the auction itself, but were withheld and acquired only in March 1827. He refers to the annotated copy of the sale's catalogue in the RMO Archives (no. 3.1/3), which has a remark on the fly-leaf likewise occurring on the fly-leaf of a second copy, Archive 3.1/4. However, both annotations by Reuvens himself clearly state that objects not bought at the auction (but only later), have been crossed out in the catalogue – and the mummies were not crossed out. The prices added in the margin also prove that all three mummies were purchased on July 5, 1826.

smaller objects. Due to the limited budget granted him by the Ministry, he was able to buy no more than 85 objects in total, so that both buyer and seller were left equally frustrated about the outcome of the auction. Then Reuvens took an unusual step: in February 1827 he made De Lescluze an offer for an additional 17 objects (including two attractive bronzes and a number of statues and stelae), to be paid with an advance from his personal means. This finally convinced the Ministry to put more money at his disposal, so that in June 1828 Reuvens succeeded in acquiring the remainder of 595 items for the Leiden collection (mainly smaller objects, such as scarabs and amulets, jewellery, more bronzes and vases, shabtis, and wooden objects). Instead of the 60.000 Dutch florins initially estimated by De Lescluze, the whole lot had not cost the RMO more than 8.000.[53]

3.2. De Lescluze's three mummies

In the auction catalogue, the three mummies are described in Chapter 12: *Momies et objets momisés* (fig. 9).[54] Upon arrival in the museum, they received the inventory numbers L.XII.1–3 (with the L referring to Lescluze, the Roman number to the chapter, and the sequence numbers to the proper entries in the sale's catalogue, as for all other objects purchased from De Lescluze). Mummy L.XII.1 was contained in a painted wooden coffin and a cartonnage mummy-sheath, both inscribed for a man Khonsuemma'a[kheru], and datable to mid-late Dynasty XXII (*c.* 850–712 BC) according to Taylor.[55] In the auction catalogue, it was mentioned as a female mummy, but upon radiological evidence it is definitely male as one would expect from the name. The second mummy (inv. L.XII.2, see below) is stated there to belong to a man with two coffins, one of wood and the other of cartonnage. The third mummy (inv. L.XII.3) is described as a female with two coffins, of which the exterior one is of wood; there seems to be a line missing from the printed text in the catalogue, referring to the inner cartonnage sheath of this mummy.[56] Both coffin and cartonnage are inscribed for a singer of Amun, Panesy, dated to early-middle Dynasty XXII (*c.* 900–800 BC) by Taylor, but since the mummy is definitely female it may have been added by the dealers instead of the original one.[57]

Because L.XII.2 is the mummy of Djedhor which forms the object of the present study, we shall quote the full entry from the sale's catalogue here (including some mistakes in grammar and orthography):

> *No. 2. Un momie d'homme à deux caisses , la plus grande 80 ½ de long en bois de sycomore recouvert de stuc colorié partout en scènes , et hiéroglyphes ; le seconde caisse ayant été ouverte en dessous est en carton mâché comme dessous, à découpures en divers endroits, ayant, le masque doré et quelques figures des scènes ; longueur 6 5/12 , la face un peu écrasée et mutilée.*

According to an annotation in ink, doubtless made by Reuvens, in the copy of the catalogue kept in the RMO archives, the mummy in question was acquired for 225 Dutch guilders – considerably less than the two other specimens, which were obviously more appreciated because of their better condition. All the same Reuvens found reasons to complain in a letter to De Lescluze of July 27:[58]

> *Mummy no. 3 has doubtlessly been opened from the back but then sown together again in a most coarse manner. No. 1 is under strong suspicion of likewise having been opened but again retouched in paint. I have the impression of clearly recognizing a French brush in the repainted area.*

It is remarkable that he found nothing to say about mummy no. 2, which had its own problems of conservation and authenticity, as we shall see in the next chapter.

53 For a detailed report of this sale, with references to the pertinent documents in the RMO Archives, see Raven, in: Ter Keurs/Wirtz 2018, 67–71. Cf. www.archieven.rmo.nl/wp-content/object_files/003.pdf#page=426–427 (letter d.d. 13 March 1825), www.archieven.rmo.nl/wp-content/object_files/004.pdf#page=95–97 and 203–204 (d.d. 18 August 1826 and 25 April 1827), and www.archieven.rmo.nl/wp-content/object_files/005.pdf#page=160 (d.d. 4 August 1828).

54 Anonymous 1826, 35–36. Illustrated in Raven 1993, 40, fig. 54.

55 Raven/Taconis 2005, 91–94, cat. 3; cf. Taylor, in: Strudwick/Taylor 2003, 101–102, Type 2.

56 Added in black ink by Reuvens in the specimen of the catalogue kept in the RMO Archives (archive no. 3.1.3, here Fig. 9).

57 Raven/Taconis 2005, 87–90, cat. 2; cf. Taylor, in: Strudwick/Taylor 2003, 101–102, Type 1.

58 Quoted in Raven 1993, 40. Cf. https://archieven.rmo.nl/wp-content/object_files/004.pdf#page=89.

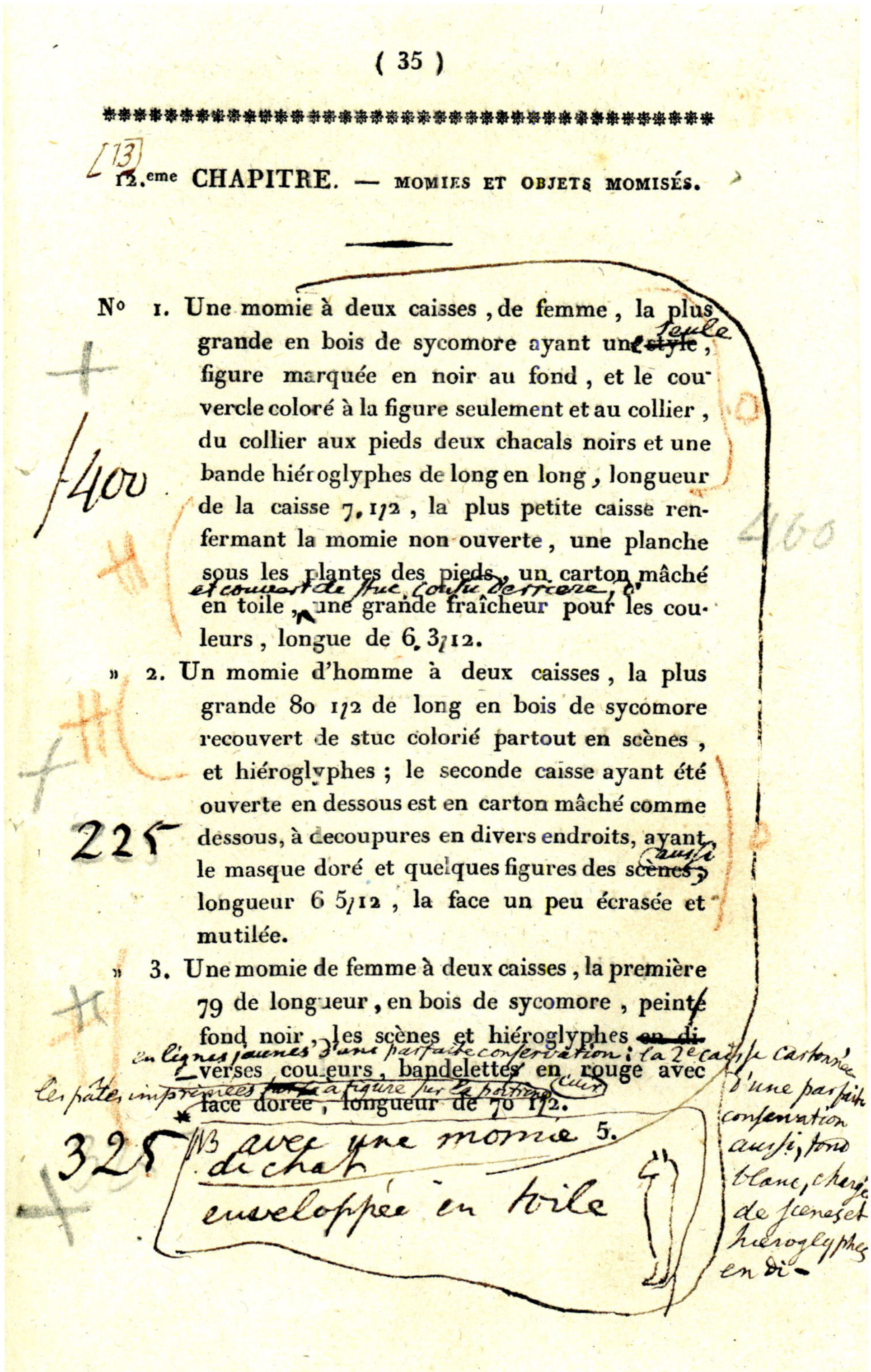
(35)

12.eme CHAPITRE. — MOMIES ET OBJETS MOMISÉS.

No 1. Une momie à deux caisses, de femme, la plus grande en bois de sycomore ayant une style, figure marquée en noir au fond, et le couvercle coloré à la figure seulement et au collier, du collier aux pieds deux chacals noirs et une bande hiéroglyphes de long en long, longueur de la caisse 7, 1/2, la plus petite caisse renfermant la momie non-ouverte, une planche sous les plantes des pieds, un carton mâché en toile, une grande fraîcheur pour les couleurs, longue de 6, 3/12.

» 2. Un momie d'homme à deux caisses, la plus grande 80 1/2 de long en bois de sycomore recouvert de stuc colorié partout en scènes, et hiéroglyphes; le seconde caisse ayant été ouverte en dessous est en carton mâché comme dessous, à decoupures en divers endroits, ayant le masque doré et quelques figures des scènes, longueur 6 5/12, la face un peu écrasée et mutilée.

» 3. Une momie de femme à deux caisses, la première 79 de longueur, en bois de sycomore, peint fond noir, les scènes et hiéroglyphes en diverses couleurs, bandelettes en rouge avec face dorée, longueur de 70 1/2.

Fig. 9. Page 35 of the Lescluze sale's catalogue with the entries on the three mummies (Archives RMO).

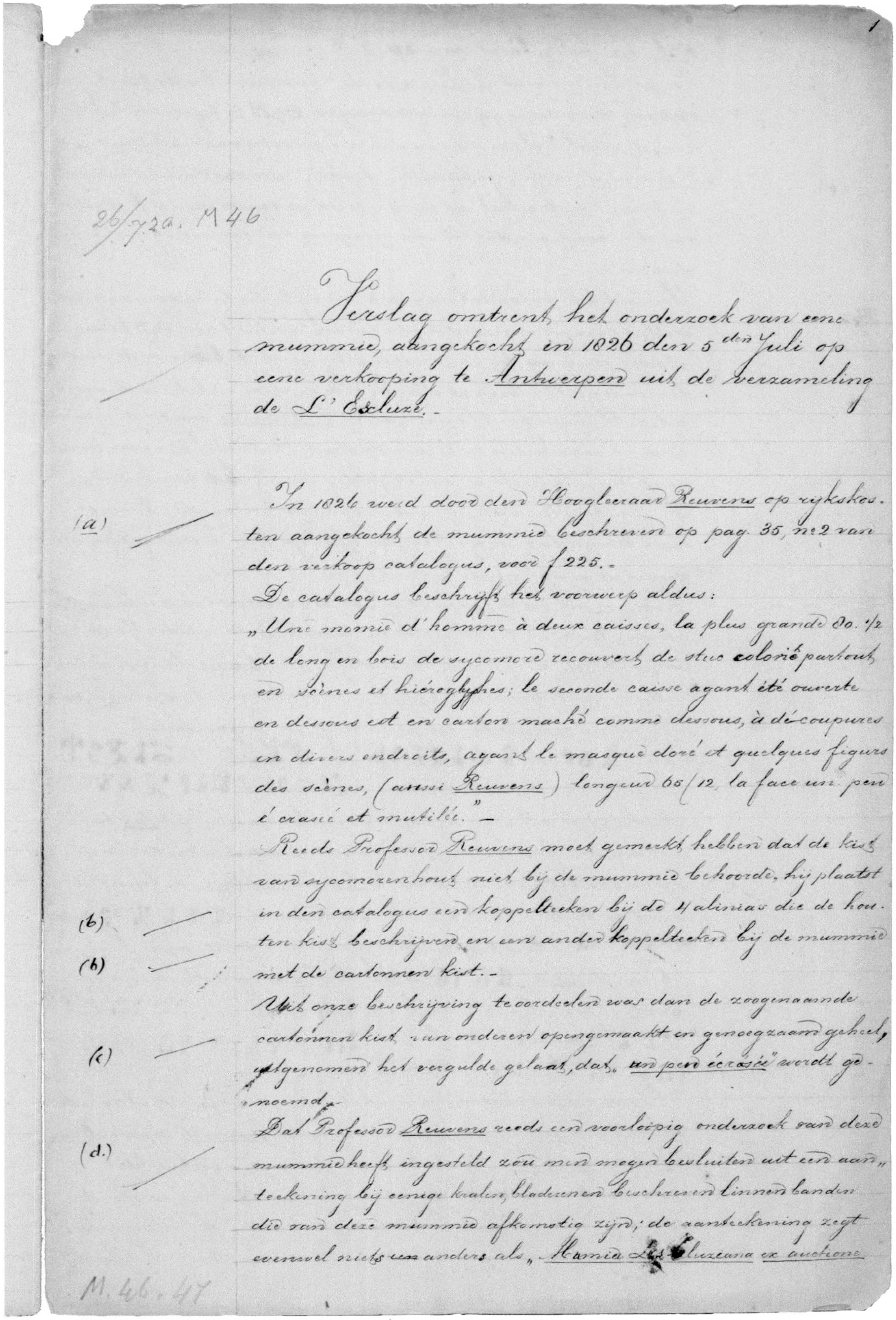

1

26/72a. M46

Verslag omtrent het onderzoek van eene mummie, aangekocht in 1826 den 5den Juli op eene verkooping te Antwerpen uit de verzameling de L'Escluze.-

(a) In 1826 werd door den Hoogleeraar Reuvens op rijkskosten aangekocht de mummie beschreven op pag. 35, no 2 van den verkoop catalogus, voor f 225.-

De catalogus beschrijft het voorwerp aldus:

„Une momie d'homme à deux caisses, la plus grande 80. 1/2 de long en bois de sycomore recouvert de stuc colorié partout en scènes et hiéroglyphes; la seconde caisse ayant été ouverte en dessous est en carton maché comme dessous, à découpures en divers endroits, ayant le masque doré et quelques figures des scènes, (aussi Reuvens) longeur 65/12, la face un peu écrasé et mutilée."-

(b) (b) Reeds Professor Reuvens moet gemerkt hebben dat de kist van sycomorenhout niet bij de mummie behoorde, hij plaatst in den catalogus een koppelteeken bij de 4 alineas die de houten kist beschrijven en een ander koppelteeken bij de mummie met de cartonnen kist.-

(c) Uit onze beschrijving te oordeelen was dan de zoogenaamde cartonnen kist van onderen opengemaakt en genoegzaam geheel, uitgenomen het vergulde gelaat, dat „un peu écrasé" wordt genoemd.-

(d.) Dat Professor Reuvens reeds een voorloopig onderzoek van deze mummie heeft ingesteld zou men mogen besluiten uit een aan„teekening bij eenige kralen, bladeren beschreven linnen banden die van deze mummie afkomstig zijn; de aanteekening zegt evenwel niets anders als „Mumia [illegible] Eluzeana ex auctione

M. 46. 47.

Fig. 10. Page 1 of the *procès-verbal* of the 1878 autopsy (Archives RMO).

Chapter 4

The 1878 autopsy

4.1. Documentation and remains

In the annual report of the RMO concerning the year 1878, mention is made of the autopsy on an Egyptian mummy by Willem Pleyte, then curator of the museum, and of the various objects found in and on the mummy in question.[59] This autopsy has never been published, though a detailed *procès-verbal* of this event has been preserved in the museum's archives (Fig. 10).[60] Excerpts and partial translations of this precious document have been quoted in a number of catalogues on the Leiden mummy collections,[61] but it has never been published in full. The report contains a wealth of detailed observations, and gives rise to a number of interesting conclusions on various aspects of Egyptian mummification. Some of these have already been summed up in the previous catalogues in question, but much more can be said about this matter. Therefore, we shall here present an English translation of the entire *procès-verbal*.[62]

This will be followed by a detailed scrutiny of all the items recovered from this mummy during the autopsy, which were carefully described and properly labelled by Pleyte, pasted on cardboard or white paper where this helped their preservation, and finally registered in the museum's inventory books.[63] These meticulous procedures ensured that the mummy – which does not exist any longer and was doubtless de-accessioned after the end of the analysis – can today still be reconstructed at least on paper. Moreover, it can be identified as the remains of a distinguished Theban priest who lived during the early Ptolemaic Period and was buried with great pomp on the west bank of the Nile. Though no report appears to have been made of its archaeological discovery, we can make an estimated guess regarding his burial place and are able to suggest the names of those persons who may have been involved in this find.

4.2. The mummy ensemble before the dissection

As we have seen above, the mummy which was Pleyte's object of study had been bought by the RMO director Caspar Reuvens in Antwerp, at the auction of the collection of Jean-Baptiste De Lescluze in 1826.[64] Upon arrival in Leiden, it was registered under inventory number L.XII.2. When acquired, the mummy was enclosed in two coffins. The exterior one (in fact an interior coffin of another set, in view of its dimensions) is mummiform,

59 Leemans 1879, 48–50.

60 Archives RMO, 6.4.3/3 *sub* 2.1.1 (box C93).

61 Raven 1993, 60–65 (here the event is dated to 1876, an error which could be corrected in the 2nd edition); Raven/Taconis 2005, 29–30; Raven, in: Ter Keurs/Wirtz 2018, 172–173.

62 Below, § 5.2.

63 *Inventaris van het Rijks Museum van Oudheden te Leiden, no. 11: Oktober 1878 t/m Maart 1882*, pages 13–15 (= RMO Archives 1.1/11).

64 *Supra*, § 3.1.

made of wood and inscribed for a man Irhapiaut who does not wield any titles (now registered as L.XII.2-b. See Fig. 11).[65] It is of a rather rare type with a lid painted with scenes and inscriptions in various horizontal registers and a case with a large image of Sokaris flanked by Isis and Nephthys; the edge of the case has a decorative net pattern with rosettes. This type of coffin is known from a number of parallels which can be dated to the XXIVth–XXVth Dynasty (736–655 BC),[66] and accordingly has no connection with the mummy and cartonnage which it enclosed, which bear a different name and manifest a style of a later period. It must have been added by the art dealers in order to make up a more attractive item for sale.

The inner 'coffin' is in fact a mummy-sheath made of cartonnage mentioning a certain Djedhor as its owner (inv. L.XII.2-d. See Figs. 13–16). Because of the different name and the divergent art style, the coffin and cartonnage clearly did not belong together. We shall see below that during the autopsy Pleyte found proof that the mummy belongs with the cartonnage (and not with the coffin), and is therefore that of a priest Djedhor, the son of Neferibre and Takerheb. However, this observation was not made until 1878, or half a century after the mummy's acquisition by Reuvens. After a cursory inspection of the mummy, Reuvens seems to have put some loose parts of this ensemble (notably inscribed mummy wrappings, beads, and leaf garlands) in a separate box.[67] With all the purchases pouring into the museum during the following years, he did not have more time to spend on a more detailed scrutiny of Djedhor's mummy.

Reuvens died in 1835, a few years before the RMO managed to acquire a suitable building for exhibiting its collections. It was not until 1838 that the museum finally opened its doors. Two years later, a first catalogue of the Egyptian collections was published by the new director, Conrad Leemans.[68] Here the mummy set received the following catalogue numbers: M 45 for the coffin of Irhapiaut (which will not be discussed in the following), M 46 for the cartonnage of Djedhor, and M 47 for the mummy.[69] The cartonnage was here described as already being in fragments: *Fragmens d'un Cartonnage travaillé à jour, et ayant renfermé la momie d'un défunt nommé ... dsja-ho*. This also suggests that the remains of the mummy had already been taken out of the cartonnage and were kept separately. The mummy itself is just mentioned (*Momie de ....dsja-ho*) but not described, which might be an indication that its condition was already rather poor at the time.

The condition of the mummy would deteriorate rather drastically in the course of the following decennia, as a result of the damp environment of the museum building, about which Leemans used to complain in an endless litany in the successive annual reports covering this period.[70] As a result of these problems, quite a number of mummies and mummy parts had to be removed from the collections. The autopsy on the mummy of Djedhor in 1878 was probably executed as a last means to investigate an object that would be de-accessioned soon after. This explains that the body parts remaining after the autopsy can no longer be found in the collections today. It is different for the textiles, amulets and other apparel of the mummy, items which were registered under new numbers after the autopsy and which still form part of the Leiden collections.

65 See https://www.rmo.nl/en/collection/search-collection/?term=&department=&object=&period=&material=&place=&inventory=L.XII.2-b. Cf. C. Sheikholeslami, in: Amenta/Guichard 2017, 488 (no. 09). For the name, see Ranke 1935–1959, I.40.4, II.343.

66 Cf. Greco 2015, 176–177, cat. 217–218 (Turin, Museo Egizio, inv. nos. S. 5226/1a–b and S. 5229/a–b: coffins of Harwa); Gasse 1996, 203–205, pls. 55–57; C. Sheikholeslami, in: Amenta/Guichard 2017, 487 with pl. 4, cf. table 3 (Vatican, Museo Gregoriano Egizio, inv. 25007: anonymous coffin); Melbourne, National Gallery of Victoria, inv. D 144–1982 (see https://www.ngv.vic.gov.au/explore/collection/work/56666: coffin case of Irthoreru).

67 Leemans 1879, 48–49. See also the *procès-verbal*, § 5.2 below, page 1; Appendix 1, notes *d-e*.

68 For Leemans, see above, § 1.3, n. 14 with Fig. 4.

69 Leemans 1840, 178–180.

70 Cf. Raven 1993, 56.

Fig. 11a–b. Coffin of Irhapiaut (RMO, inv. L.XII.2-b), lid and case.

Chapter 5

The *procès-verbal*

5.1. Introduction

The full text of the autopsy report (= Archives RMO, box C93, 6.4.3/3 *sub* 2.1.1) is here given in an English translation. The original is in Dutch and contains a number of misspellings, inaccurate quotations, and corrections. All this has been silently emended here, with the occasional word added between square brackets, and only here and there a footnote has been added to comment on specific points.

It should be noted that Pleyte's numbering of the various paragraphs is rather chaotic. The first section of his text (on p. 2) is numbered '1' but should be understood as referring to Leemans cat. M 46, i.e. the mummy cartonnage. Separate paragraphs then describe what once lay on top of, or directly under this cartonnage (sections '46a–d' on pp. 3–6). Then follows the mummy itself ('M 47' on p. 6), with a proper heading for the torso ('M 47b') but omitting a similar heading for the preceding description of the feet and lower legs (*M 47a on p. 6), and omitting a proper section at the very end for the head (*M 47c, entries 37–38 on p. 10). Individual finds are numbered 1–6 for the feet, then 1–36 for the torso, with nos. 37–38 referring mainly to the head.

The original has been written in black ink on 15 numbered pages of 34.5 × 21.6 cm. The text shows Pleyte's fluent handwriting (Fig. 10); some corrections in pencil have been added in another hand, doubtless by Leemans. The latter also compiled four pages of comments (*Aanmerkingen*) dated 4 July 1878, in the form of loose notes which refer to the letters added by him in the left-hand margin of the original *procès-verbal*.[71] Pleyte reacted to this in a three-page document (*Opmerkingen*).[72] Both documents are kept with the *procès-verbal* in the RMO Archives, together with a loose sheet with pencil notes regarding the mummy, apparently made during the autopsy itself. We shall refer to these documents where it is relevant.

71 Cf. below, Appendix 1.
72 Below, Appendix 2.

5.2. Translation of the *procès-verbal*

[page 1]

Account of the autopsy of a mummy, purchased on July 5th, 1826
at an auction of the collection De Lescluze in Antwerp

In 1826 professor Reuvens bought, at the expense of the state, the mummy described in the auction catalogue on page 35, no. 2, for the amount of 225 florins. The catalogue describes this object as follows:[73] 'Une momie d'homme à deux caisses, la plus grande 80 ½ de long en bois de sycomore recouvert de stuc colorié partout en scènes, et hiéroglyphes; la seconde caisse ayant été ouverte en dessous est en carton mâché comme dessous,[74] à découpures en divers endroits, ayant le masque doré et quelques figures des scènes (aussi Reuvens);[75] longueur 6 5/12, la face un peu écrasée et mutilée.'
Professor Reuvens must already have noticed that the coffin of sycomore wood does not belong with the mummy. He puts a dash in front of the four paragraphs describing the wooden coffin and another dash for the mummy with its cartonnage coffin.[76] Judging from the catalogue entry the so-called cartonnage had been opened below[77] and was practically complete, with exception of the gilt face which is called 'un peu écrasée'. That Professor Reuvens already undertook a provisional investigation of this mummy can be concluded from a written note accompanying various beads, leaves, and inscribed linen bandages from this mummy. However, this note merely states 'Mumia LesCluziana ex auctione

[page 2]

1826 in Julio Catal. cap XII.2.'
In which condition Dr Leemans knew the mummy can be seen from his 1840 description in *Description raisonnée*, page 179, no. M 46. He mentions the second coffin as 'Fragmens d'un cartonnage travaillé à jour', whereas the first one is described under the [name] of its former owner. This indicates that the exterior mummy cover had by then already been torn to pieces, and that the rear (mentioned in the catalogue as 'le dessous'), which had also been provided with openwork decoration, was completely missing.[78] Presumably the rear part showed few recognizable details and it may have had areas which had been charred and decayed by the bitumen. After a previous occasion when I investigated the texts on the bandages, stored them in their proper order, and later reconstructed the garlands from the loose leaves, Dr Leemans ordered me to further investigate and unwrap the mummy.[79] Now that the various parts have been investigated, I shall describe them one by one.

1. Exterior cover of the mummy, consisting of several layers of linen sheets, stuck together and with some parts cut out and showing the underlying cover. On top of the head is a depiction of a beetle flying with extended wings, between the front legs a solar disk positioned centrally over the forehead, the rear legs terminating in uraeus serpents

73 The quotation is from: Anonymous 1826, 35 (see Fig. 9). The measurements are in inches.
74 Read *dessus*, as this is a reference to no. 1 of the catalogue which also mentions cartonnage parts.
75 Reuvens added 'aussi' to indicate that also some scenes were gilt.
76 For the 'dashes' see the discussion below, Appendices 1 and 2, note *b*.
77 Below, i.e. at the rear. The catalogue entry is in fact ambivalent: does it imply that the cartonnage was originally open at the rear (which is correct: see below, § 7.1), or rather that is was opened in recent times (as Leemans and Pleyte seem to understand)?
78 This is not explicitly stated by Leemans, and is in fact incorrect.
79 Pencil note by Leemans in the margin: 'in my view, there is no need to mention the order to do so.'

provided with the white and red crowns of Egypt; the entire design in an oval frame, surrounded by a very fragmentary text in hieroglyphic writing.

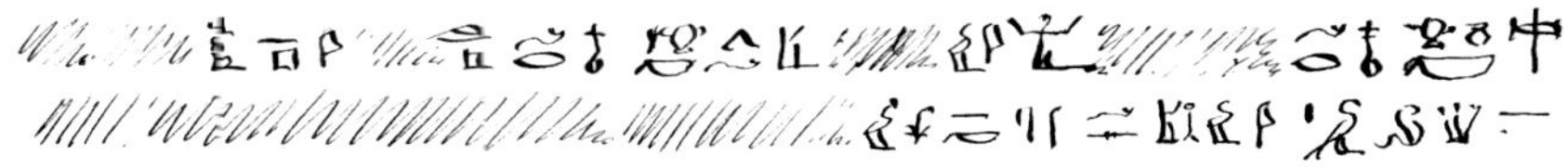

The head cover hangs down behind, painted in brown with a *djed* sign surmounted by a human bust (the image of Sokaris-Osiris), flanked by a standing Isis and Nephthys in adoring position, with a caption below:
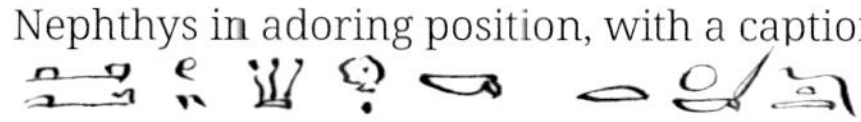 'Both my hands are behind you in order to protect you forever.' Above the Isis 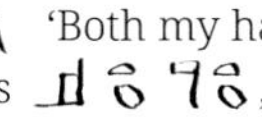, behind the Isis part of a text in hieroglyphic writing.[80]

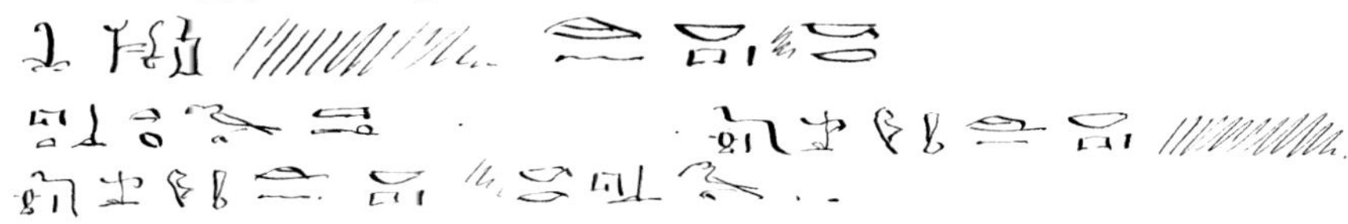

On the chest an extensive decoration consisting of a collar and a gilt flying falcon with human head, plus a gilt pectoral depicting Osiris, Isis and Nephthys. Below the collar a winged falcon or beetle of which the main part is lost, just as the hieroglyphic captions above. Underneath, the sky goddess adorned with a solar disk, kneeling on one knee and winged,

[page 3]

with above a hieroglyphic caption in eight short columns, of which only the name 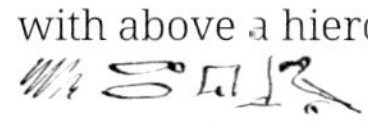 can be read.
Below, a funerary bier with the soul flying above and the four canopic jars underneath, the goddesses Isis and Nephthys to either side with the four funerary genii (two mummiform, two wearing a *shenti*). In front of Isis and Nephthys there is also a serpent on a base, with a solar disk on the head.
Below, several lotus flowers stacked on top of each other, flanked by two Osiris figures, with next to them two goddesses (presumably Isis and Nephthys) and the gods Horus and Thoth with the symbolic eye. Underneath a wide column with a gilt inscription for the deceased extends down to the feet, though completely fragmented and illegible. This is flanked to either side by two rows of funerary genii, both clothed and mummiform ones.
Also to either side 4 seated male deities with human heads, followed by the falcon standing on the sign , holding the sceptre in one claw and adorned with a solar disk on the head, preceded by a caption 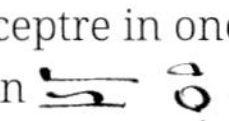 and the cartouche Osiris 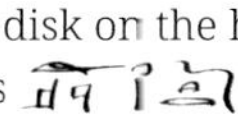 on one side, and on the other side 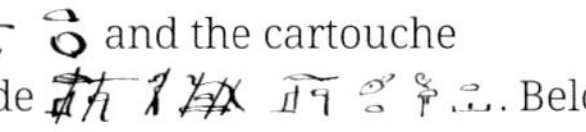. Below this depiction are the images of Apheru[81] with the caption 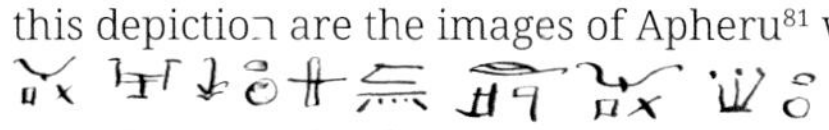. Above this depiction a wriggling serpent with three heads, all with solar disks. All these representations are separated by bands of flowers or coloured squares. On the soles of the feet two Asiatics, their hands bound behind their backs and a rope around their necks, with the caption 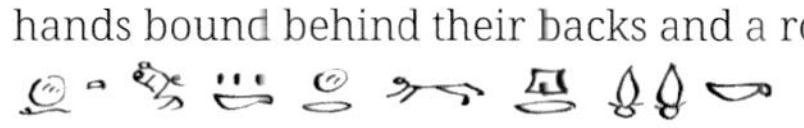. 'your enemies fall under your feet.'
The concomitant texts prove, therefore, that the cover belonged to the mummy of a royal scribe Ishar, son of the housewife Kerheb.

80 Probably, this text consisted of protective formulas in several lines or columns, all ending with the names of the deceased and his mother (the only part still legible at the time).

81 Clearly referring to the two Wepwawet jackals, whose name was apparently still imperfectly understood at the time. Cf. McClintock/Strong 1870, entry for 'Apheru'.

46a. The various beads must have belonged to a net of the type which adorned several other mummies. This net has disintegrated and cannot be reconstructed for lack of information.

46b. The leaves of *mimusops kummel* have been reconstructed to form two wreaths, together with the strings made of *doum* palm leaf, as described in the inventory Am 11–13. It seems that this mummy (as several others) had one wreath on the head and another

[page 4]
on the chest.

46c. The previous unwrapping[82] produced the fragments of linen bandages inscribed with various texts and the parts of larger shrouds. The first concern two kinds of texts and were probably wrapped in parallel bands around the body in their full length. Some parts still stuck to the already badly damaged mummy. Together, they are sufficiently long to wrap the entire mummy in a parallel pattern, even in double rows. Only 5 fragments are about one metre long; the other fragments have been fitted together according to clues in the texts, or on the basis of matching stains.

fragment 1. 'Recitation by Osiris, first of the west, the great god, lord of Abydos, and Isis, the divine mother, and Nephthys, the divine sister, and Anubis, who is in the place of embalming, first of the divine booth, that he may give beef and poultry to you.'
fragment 2. '... Osiris, first of the west, lord of Abydos. Isis the divine, Anubis, who is in the place of embalming, first of the divine booth, may he give veneration with Re, may he give abundance ...'
fragment 3. '... the great, Anubis, who is in the place of embalming, first of the divine booth, may he give an abode ...'
fragment 4. '... Nephthys, the divine sister, and Anubis, who is in the place of embalming, may he give bread and beer, beef and poultry, wine and milk, flowers and clothing to the Osiris Tsaher, justified, the son of Neferibre.'
fragment 5. '... may he give veneration with Re and abundance with Osiris, first of the west, lord of Abydos, to the divine Isis and Nephthys ...'
fragments 6–18 provide similar phrases.
fragment 19. '... the royal scribe, royal scribe of Nekheb. The divine ... scribe of the temple of Amun? Tsahor' 
fragment 20. '... justified, son of Kerheb, justified.'
fragments 21-22. '... scribe of Wati ? and Nekheb 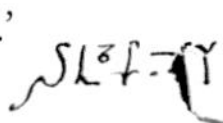 Tsaher, son of Neferibre ... the deceased, son of the housewife Kerheb, justified,

[page 5]
may he live forever. Recitation by the Osiris Tsaher, justified, born to', etc.
fragments 23–51. Similar captions.
The *fragments 52–54 and 55* deal with a different subject and seem to contain exclamations; the text is badly written and therefore hard to translate.
Fragments 56 and 57–70 provide the same as the above-mentioned fragments.
The other bandages contain portions of the Book of the Dead, such as:
Fragments 71–77. Chapter 1.1–5 with small omissions.
Fragments 78–81. Chapter 2.

82 This refers to what on pages 5–6 (*sub* 46d) is mentioned as a partial unwrapping done by Reuvens. See also below, Appendix 1, note *e*, where it is stated that Reuvens collected these loose materials in a wooden box with a glass lid.

[*Fragment*] 82. Chapter 5, partially.
Fragments 83–87. Chapter 6, partially.
Fragments 88–91. Chapter 7.1–4.
Fragments 92–93. Fragments of texts like 1–70, continuing with a line containing Chapter 18:10 of the Book of the Dead.
These inscriptions indicate that the deceased fulfilled the position of royal scribe for the goddesses Uati and Nekheb and that he was the son of Neferibre. This name is known as the prenomen of King Psamtik II – a fact to which we shall recur later on.

46d. The fragmentary bandages also comprise 12 pieces with the depiction of mummiform figures (6 with human faces and 6 with uraeus heads), possibly a representation of the 12 nightly hours, and a vignette from the Book of the Dead representing 'the deceased transferring the phoenix heron in a barque'. Also the almost life-size figure of Osiris as judge of the netherworld; this last textile is entered under number O 48 in the catalogue by Dr Leemans, which states:[83]
'Pièce très fine, sur laquelle sont tracés la tête et une partie du corps d'Osiris .... le devant de la coiffure orné d'une barque avec la grue.'
Since the provenance of this piece was unknown to Dr Leemans, this indicates that the provisional investigation of the mummy was not started by him but by Professor Reuvens. I found part of the face (nose, mouth and chin) and the shepherd staff and part of the collar among the above-mentioned bandages. If we compare the vignette from the Book of the Dead with what is represented on top of the headdress,[84] the fact that this textile belongs with the other bandages is beyond all doubt. Hereafter, we shall describe the remains of other shrouds, for instance with an Isis and Nephthys. Probably,

[page 6]
these bandages and this cover could be removed piece by piece, until the Professor hit the almost impenetrable layer of pitch which covered the rest of the body. Apparently, he started his investigation at the head, and since this did not produce a lot, then continued at the feet. Indeed, those were the parts which clearly showed traces of previous investigation when I myself received the mummy, as will be proved by the further report.

M 47. Upon reception of the mummy for my autopsy, it had been broken in three parts: the head, the torso down to the knees, and the legs. The breaks revealed the interior was charred due to pitch. I started my autopsy with the legs, from which the layer of pitch had been removed, while the feet dropped off as soon as the first bandages were unwrapped. This autopsy indicated that the wrappings could be regarded as a continuation of those on the upper body. After some unwrapping I encountered an overall cover in the form of a single textile which enclosed the legs as a stocking and extended over the feet.
Anklets of linen coated in stucco and then painted in brown and gold had been applied around the ankles, stretching to the rear side of the leg where they were secured by a string (see 47a 1 and 2).
Soles had been fixed under the feet (see 3 and 4), by means of a string running next to the big toe, passing through the soles behind, and bound to the feet on the upper face of the insteps (see 5). Otherwise a bandage inscribed with the sign of a footsole was wrapped around the foot (see 6), indicating that the wrappings used for the

83 The quotation is from Leemans 1840, 199.
84 This refers to the similarity of the barque with a phoenix, probably a vignette of BD 100, occurring both as a loose vignette and as a depiction on the crown of the large Osiris image.

various limbs were probably marked. We shall mention the other marked bandages later. The nails of the feet were gilt, as could be seen on the mummy after the removal of some layers of wrappings.
After further unwrapping I encountered very thin and fine linen which proved to be the first mummy wrapping. On one foot the flesh was very well recognizable, though as hard as glass due to the infiltration of pitch and balm, and crumbling at the slightest compression. On the other foot the byssus cover can still be detected. Otherwise nothing can be reported about the legs, apart from the fact that on one leg the flesh has rather crumbled off, while the other has preserved the wrapping of fine byssus.

47b The Torso.
At thigh level on the rear side of the torso, parts of the pitch coating had been taken away. Small portions of the inscribed bandages still adhered to the edges of the cavity; these were

[page 7]
removed and mounted on paper. They consisted of narrow bands with the same texts as on the outer wrappings, so that a complete layer of narrow bands seems to have been lost in the thick coating of pitch, or even a double layer because they consisted of two layers, one under the other (see 1–6 upper layer, 7–10 lower layer).
Next, I tried to remove the pitch coating from the upper side of the mummy. I broke off by hand a part of this coating from a cavity above the knee. Then I noticed the lower end of a text on papyrus, rolled up many times and protruding from the break, enclosed by the pitch on all sides and broken off. With the utmost care I then removed the complete right femur, which could be lifted from the rear and slipped out of its socket; after that the left femur with the lower part of the torso, so that the lower end of the papyrus became visible up to half its length. At its lower face (the side which had rested against the body) could still be seen a fragment of the inscribed bandages. After this, we removed the arms and the thorax.
11. The papyrus was sawn out of the covering, unrolled, and stuck to vegetable paper; I shall give a description below.[85] Immediately under the papyrus lay the inscribed bandages mentioned under 1–10, covering a fine linen shroud with several small vignettes (no. 12) such as:

a. A vulture with phallus.
b. A uraeus on stairs.
c. A serpent in a shrine.
d. An unrecognizable figure, perhaps depiction of a *shenti* garment.
e. Part of a crocodile.

Presumably these include:

f. Part of a woman or goddess.
g. Lower part of a man.
h. Part of a woman.

Everything polychrome.
13. Parts of a shroud with the image of a goddess, presumably Nephthys.
14. Part of a shroud with the image of a King, at least its lower part suggests so.
15. A painted shroud mentioned with respect to the unwrapping of the legs,[86] but which will have covered the entire body,

85 Pages 11–15 of the original report.
86 This is incorrect: this shroud including vignettes of various gods and goddesses was mentioned in entry 46d, concerning fragments already removed by Reuvens and temporarily stored in a separate box (see below, ns. 136–138).

[page 8]

with polychrome depictions of the figures of several gods and goddesses, but now unrecognizable due to the infiltration of the bitumen.

16. On top of this was fixed a necklace, with a coloured string slung around the neck and a centrepiece stuck to the chest, consisting of:

a. a string of which the knot has been preserved.
b. a bulb of garlic with its stem.
c. three blue faience amulets: bow-knots of belts  .
d. four ditto amulets of the stairs  .
e. three ditto amulets: tassels  .
f. four ditto funerary genii.
g. three heart vases of various stone.
h. one gilt faience scarab.
i. ditto figurine of Isis.
k. ditto figurine of Nephthys.
l. ditto bunch of grapes (?).
m. ditto heart vase.
n. haematite head-rest.
o. gilt faience *djed*.
p. ditto bow-knot of belt.
q. ditto mummy.
r. gilt faience *aper* sign (bunch of onions and flowers).
s. ditto falcon.
t. ditto sacred eye.
u. ditto tassel amulet.
v. ditto squatting falcon.
w. ditto column.
x. two ivory sacred eyes.
y. tassel ornament of ivory.

17. Presumably, the mummy decoration at this level of the wrappings consisted of a painted face, of which nothing can now be seen; the addition of armlets and wristlets, fragments of which have been preserved; the gilding of the nails, which is still visible; the adhesion of an ivory bezel onto the ring finger, as if the finger was adorned with a ring (see 18); and the placing of an onion or rather garlic bulb in the hand (see 19). The right arm was bent over the chest, with the hand lying flat; the left one was placed crosswise over the former, with the hand holding

[page 9]

the onion and wearing the ivory bezel.

20. Linen braces were slung around the neck, crossing over the chest and inscribed with the titles and name of the deceased.

21. A shroud with gilt nipples, followed by a filling of small pieces of textile, and

22. Parallel bands, one with a demotic text [23] .

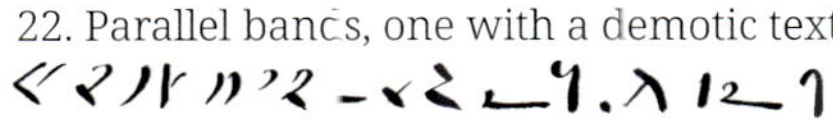

24. Filling of small pieces of textile, and artificial nipples made of textile.

25. Filling and cross-bands.

26. Shroud with a drawing of the image of Isis holding a sacred eye.

27. Girdle of braces and cross-bands which were without inscriptions.

28. Three shrouds.

29. Scroll of papyrus inscribed in hieroglyphic writing of which practically nothing remains. The texts have been written vertically. The scroll was attached to the left side of the neck.[87]

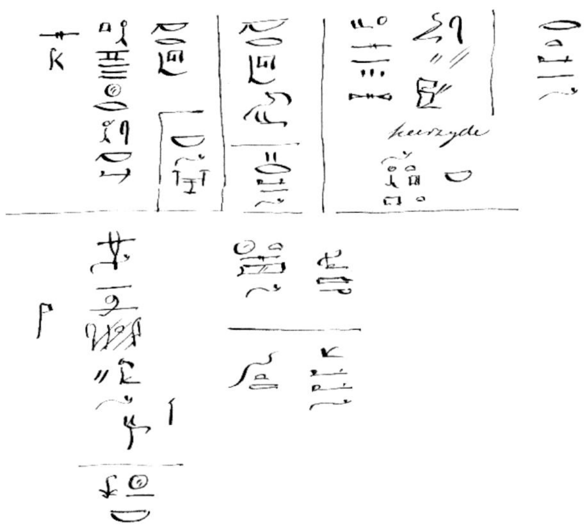

Since the name Kerheb occurs twice in these texts, we can safely assume that the text was written for the deceased and contained a incantation.
30. Wrapping with bandages of fine byssus.
31. Samples of linen with which the mummy has been wrapped and which helped to fill the body in places.
32. Samples of sewing.
33. Samples of mending.

[page 10]
34. Bandage which has been stuck with resin to the underlying fill.
34[bis]. Bandages with marks such as 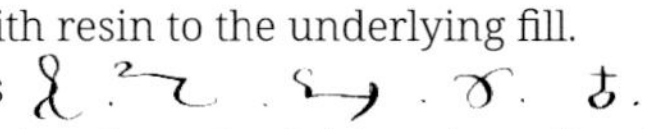
35. Several samples of bandages, all taken from the thighs where they had been best preserved. One is complete, there are narrower and wider ones.
36. Circular filling, unknown from which part of the body.
37. The body has been reassembled after everything from the exterior had been removed. I took only one of the rolled pieces from the intestines and boiled it out, but this did not provide any result. The head, where on the rear the linen had been cut away down to the bone while the face was still covered with a dense layer of bandages soaked in pitch, was likewise boiled out in order to verify whether the eyes or mouth had been provided with amulets, but this did not produce anything. The skull lacks one molar, whereas the four wisdom teeth are only partially intact. The phallus had been wrapped separately and was bound to the scrotum which was also wrapped separately; both had been laid against the left thigh.
38. Pitch employed in embalming, molten down and leaked out of the head by heating.

87 The Dutch word 'keerzijde' occurring on the text copy means 'reverse', implying the papyrus was inscribed on both sides.

[page 11]

Papyrus.

Column XXVI title.

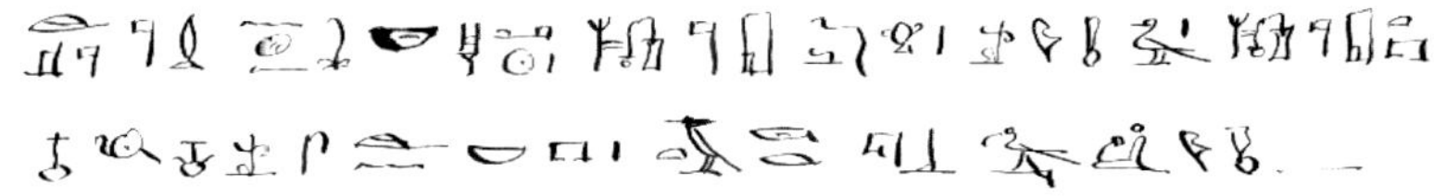

In the text.

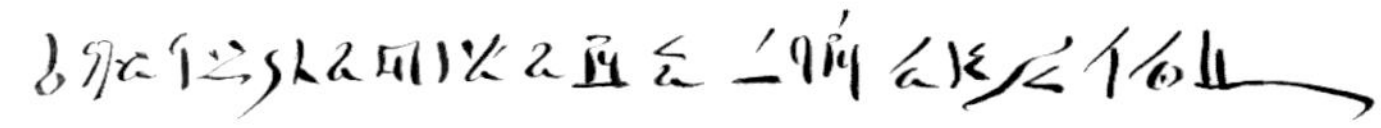

[page 12 blank]

[page 13]

Papyrus 

The first column is much damaged, wide 41 cm, high 39; polychrome vignettes, some of which painted in yellow pigment. 27 lines.

Column I, Lines 1–21	Chapter 1
Column I, Lines 21–23	Chapter 2
Column I, Lines 23–25	Chapter 3
Column I, Lines 25–27	Chapter 4
Column II rather well preserved, wide 40 cM; 28 lines.	
Column II, Line 1	Chapter 5
Column II, Lines 2–4	Chapter 6
Column II, Lines 4–7	Chapter 7
Column II, Lines 7–9	Chapter 8
Column II, Lines 9–12	Chapter 9
Column II, Lines 12–14	Chapter 10
Column II, Lines 14–17	Chapter 11
Column II, Line 17	Chapter 12 title
Column II, Lines 17–20	Chapter 14 text
Column II, Lines 20–28	Chapter 15 a-c
Column III, wide 15 cm	Chapter 16
Columns IV to VI, wide 62.5 cm, above	Chapter 18 with corrected vignettes.
Column VI, Lines 10–15	Chapter 21
Column VI, Lines 16–23	Chapter 22
Column VI, Lines 23–28	Chapter 23
Column VI, Lines 29–34	Chapter 24
Columns VII–IX, wide 57 cm.	
Column VII, Lines 1–11	Chapter 30
Column VII, Lines 11–13	Chapter 31
Column VII, Lines 13–21	Chapter 32
Column VIII, Lines 1–4	Chapter 33
Column VIII, Lines 5–8	Chapter 34
Column VIII, Lines 9–14	Chapter 35
Column VIII, Lines 15–20	Chapter 36
Column VIII, Lines 20–29	Chapter 38
Column VIII, Lines 29–35	Chapter 39
Column IX, Lines 1–9	Chapter 41

Column IX, Lines 10–15	Chapter 42 partially
Column IX, Lines 16–23	Chapter 44
Column IX, Lines 24–29	Chapter 45
Column IX, Lines 29–35	Chapter 46
Columns X–XII, wide 63.5 cm.	
Column X, Lines 1–9	Chapter 47

[page 14]

Column X, Lines 9–15	Chapter 48
Column X, Lines 16–23	Chapter 49
Column X, Lines 24–30	Chapter 50
Column X, Lines 31–35	Chapter 51
Column XI	[unknown vignette, MJR]
Column XII, vignette	Chapter 110
Columns XIII–XV, wide 51.5 cm.	
Column XIII, Lines 1–12	Chapter 111
Column XIII, Lines 13–28	Chapter 113
Column XIII, Lines 29–36	Chapter 114
Column XIV, Line 1	Chapter 114ff.
Column XIV, Lines 2–7	Chapter 117
Column XIV, Lines 8–13	Chapter 118
Column XIV, Lines 13–20	Chapter 119
Column XIV, Lines 21–25	Chapter 120
Column XIV, Lines 25–33	Chapter 121
Column XIV, Lines 34ff.	Chapter 122
Column XV	Chapter 125 a.b
Column XVI, wide 55.5 cm	Chapter 125 c
Columns XVII–XIX, wide 60 cm.	
Column XVII, Lines 1–16	Chapter 127
Column XVII, Lines 17–end	Chapter 128
Column XVIII, Lines 1–19	Chapter 129
Column XVIII, Lines 20–end	Chapter 130
Column XIX, Lines 1–17	Chapter 131
Column XIX, Lines 17–22	Chapter 132
Column XIX, Lines 22–28	Chapter 137
Column XIX, Lines 29–end	Chapter 138
Columns XX–XXV, wide 49 cm	Chapter 145
Column XXVI–XXVII, wide 60 cm	Chapter 148 vignette

The caption of lines 14–16 is largely that which is written on the bandages.

Column XXVII	Chapter 140
Columns XXVIII–XXXIV, wide 66.5 cm	Chapter 141
Columns XXXV–XXXVII, wide 49.5 cm.	
Column XXXV	Chapter 150
Column XXXVI	Chapter 149
Column XXXVII	Chapter 143
Columns XXXVIII–XXXIX, wide 56 cm.	
Column XXXVIII	Chapter 152
Column XXXIX	Chapter 144

[page 15]

Columns XL–XLI , wide 28 cm.	
Column XL	Chapters 151–152ff.
Column XLI	Chapter [unknown vignette, MJR]
Column XLII, wide 61 cm	Chapters 145 and 144
The last one double. See Column XXXIX.	
Columns XLIII–XLIV, wide 45 cm.	
Column XLIII	Chapter 161
Column XLIV	Chapter 162

The manuscript is well witten, the vignettes have been drawn in a firm hand, the text is almost undamaged except for the first column. The papyrus is very fragile and cracks when exposed to the air. It consists of two kinds, which have been stuck together at column XIX, even overlapping the vignettes and the text of the XIXth column.

The appearance of the mummy betrays it belongs to the period between the XXVth and the beginning of the XXVIth Dynasty. Compare Mariette Cat. de Boulac,[88] Birch on the unrolling of a Mummy.[89] The name Neferabre indicates the time of Psamtik II (Tsaher was a son of his).[90]
The amulets and the demotic text indicate the same period. Stylistically, the papyrus belongs to the XXVIth Dynasty, similar to Papyrus XVII and XVIII of Leiden.[91] XVII belonged to a Psamtik who lived in Memphis. The present papyrus seems to belong to a priest of Khonsu who came from Thebes.
Takorahaba or Takerheb occurs one more time on a wooden stela, present in the Leiden museum (W 19) [92] This stela likewise comes from the collection of De Lescluze (see L.IX.8)[93] and has cost 44 guilders. Probably both monuments have come up from the same family tomb.

88 Probably referring to Mariette 1864, but unclear to which object. Coffins, cartonnages, and mummies of this period are catalogued there under nos. 596–621, 728–752, 796–803.

89 Birch 1855.

90 Indeed Neferibre is the prenomen of Psamtik II (595–589 BC).

91 The reference is to Leemans 1840, 247 (cat. nos. T 17–18). Leiden T 17 (inv. AMS 19) was most recently studied by Quirke, who convincingly argues its owner was a contemporary of Ptolemy VIII (144–116 BC); see Quirke 1999, 42. Leiden T 18 (inv.no. AMS 58), on the other hand, appears indeed to date to Dynasty XXVI (see Coenen 1999, 74).

92 The catalogue reference is to Leemans 1840, 304. This stela is dated to the middle/late Ptolemaic Period (see Munro 1973, 243, *sub* Leiden XIV, 3). See *infra*, Fig. 57.

93 This inventory number is incorrect; the proper number is AH 21, which indicates the stela came from the Anastasi collection

PART II

DJEDHOR'S FUNERARY ENSEMBLE AND ITS PARALLELS

Fig. 12. Djedhor's funeral. Detail of Djedhor's Book of the Dead papyrus (RMO, inv. AL 61 vel 1).

Chapter 6

Numbering issues

In his report, Pleyte mentions several bandages, manuscripts, amulets and other objects which he removed from the decayed mummy. He gave all of them a provisional number, but the order of these numbers is most confusing. Before starting his autopsy, those objects already lying loose as a result of previous interventions in the museum were ranged with the cartonnage cover (Leemans catalogue M 46) and accordingly received numbers 46a–d. This group includes a few elements of a bead net (46a) and some leaf garlands (46b), but also part of the inscribed bandages of the mummy proper (46c) and of an Osiris shroud underneath (46d) – both of which belong in fact with the mummy itself (Leemans M 47). Then Pleyte started his own autopsy by cutting up the three parts of the broken mummy as he received it. Presumably, we have to understand that the leg part was numbered 47a, the torso 47b and the head 47c, though this is never mentioned in an explicit manner.[94] All we have is a brief description of the objects found on the legs (47a 1–6), then those from the torso (47b 1–37). Number 37 of the latter series, though, also mentions details about the head already, and number 38 exclusively relates to the head. It would therefore be logical to call these two entries 47c 1–2 instead.

When Pleyte mounted the objects found during the autopsy on cardboard, such frames or panels were provided with paper labels inscribed with his autopsy numbers. In other cases, however, no number was written on or attached to the objects, making it very difficult to identify them among the present-day museum collections. Next, these objects were entered in the inventory book of the museum.[95] Here, no reference was made to the provisional autopsy numbers, but instead the objects received new numbers AL 1–64 (AL presumably referring to Antwerp Lescluze).[96] Once again these numbers were not written on the actual objects. In the 1990s, the proper inventory numbers were entered in the digital registration of the museum's collections, but the problem of the identification of the objects could not always be solved in a satisfactory manner. In order to provide unique digital numbers, several groups of objects hitherto registered under a common number (for instance Djedhor's ensemble, inv.no. L.XII.2) had to be split up by the addition of alphabetical endings (such as L.XII.2-a). Table 1 represents an endeavour to clarify these manifold problems. The last column refers to the chapters of the present publication.

94 See already § 5.1 above.

95 *Inventaris van het Rijks Museum van Oudheden te Leiden, no. 11: Oktober 1878 t/m Maart 1882*, pages 13–15 (= RMO Archives 1.1/11).

96 For the system of inventory numbers of the RMO collections, see Raven 1992, 7–10. Before 1891, objects received letter marks referring in some manner to their acquisition. From 1891 onwards, the inventory numbers consist of a letter referring to the museum department (F = Egypt), the year and month of acquisition, and a serial number.

object	autopsy number	inventory number	catalogue number	chapter
cartonnage	-	L.XII.2-d	Leemans M 46	7
beads	M 46a	-	-	9
leaf garlands	M 46b	Am 10-b, Am 11-c, L.XII.2-g	-	8
inscribed bandages	M 46c	AL 51 vel 1–4, 6–7	Van 't Hooft 355	10
Osiris shroud	M 46d	AL 38	Leemans O 48; Van 't Hooft 149	10, 14
textile 12 deities	M 46d	AL 42	Van 't Hooft 152	10
textile phoenix boat	M 46d	AL 43	Van 't Hooft 152	10
anklets	M 47a.1–2	AL 47a–b	Van 't Hooft 159	11
foot soles	M 47a.3–4	AL 46a–b	-	11
string for foot soles	M 47a.5	-	-	11
bandage for foot	M 47a.6	-	-	11
inscribed bandages	M 47b.1–10	AL 51 vel 5	-	10, 12, 14
Book of the Dead	M 47b.11	AL 61	-	12
decorated shroud	M 47b.12 a–h	AL 44a–e	Van 't Hooft 153–157	14
shroud with Nephthys	M 47b.13	AL 39	Van 't Hooft 151	14
shroud with king	M 47b.14	AL 41	Van 't Hooft 151	14
decorated shroud	M 47b.15	AL 45a–e	Van 't Hooft 158	14
amuletic necklace	M 47b.16	AL 1–36	-	13
wristlet	M 47b.17	AL 47c	Van 't Hooft 159	11
bezel	M 47b.18	AL 37	-	13
garlic	M 47b.19	AL 63 = L.XII.2-c	-	13
linen braces	M 47b.20	?	-	14
shroud with nipples	M 47b.21	L.XII.2-l	Van 'Hooft 147	14
parallel bandages	M 47b.22	?	-	14
bandage with demotic	M 47b.23	AL 59	-	14
fill for breasts	M 47b.24	L.XII.2-l, L.XII.2-m	Van 't Hooft 147	14
fill and cross-bands	M 47b.25	AL 50a–d	Van 't Hooft 181	14
shroud with Isis	M 47b.26	AL 40	Van 't Hooft 150	14
stola	M 47b.27	?	-	14
3 shrouds	M 47b.28	L.XII.2-e–f, L.XII.2-k	Van 't Hooft 142–144	14
hieroglyphic papyrus	M 47b.29	AL 60	-	12
byssus bandages	M 47b.30	L.XII.2-a	Van 't Hooft 145	14
textile samples	M 47b.31	AL 48	Van 't Hooft 171–176	14
sewing samples	M 47b.32	AL 48	Van 't Hooft 160, 162	14
mending samples	M 47b.33	AL 48	Van 't Hooft 168–170, 177	14
bandages with resin	M 47b.34	AL 48	Van 't Hooft 166	14
bandages with marks	M 47b.34bis	AL 48	Van 't Hooft 161, 163–165, 167	14
bandages from thighs	M 47b.35	AL 49, L.XII.2-a, -j, -o	Van 't Hooft 141, 146, 179–180	14
disc (navel?)	M 47b.36	L.XII.2-i	Van 't Hooft 140	14
body/head	M 47b.37	-	-	-
resin	M 47b.38	AL 64	-	14

Table 1. Concordance of numbers of Djedhor's objects. Leemans = Leemans 1840; Van 't Hooft = Van 't Hooft *et al.* 1994; (Dutch) *vel* = 'sheet, frame'.

Chapter 7

The cartonnage

7.1. Description

As mentioned by Pleyte, the cartonnage is now in a very bad state of conservation. He had it consolidated by nailing it onto a wooden plank and covering the flaking painted surface with sheets of rice paper stuck to the original pigments. Until 1990, the rear of this support still contained a fill of newspaper fragments dated to 1877, which confirms the date of Pleyte's intervention since his autopsy of the mummy took place in 1878. The mummy-sheath was newly consolidated in 1990, when the flat wooden support was replaced by a curved one made of foamboard, the rice paper was removed, and large areas were strengthened with artificial resin and modern linen. The result is a wreck of an object, but careful inspection still betrays its former splendour (Figs. 13–15). The object received inventory number L.XII.2-d in the modern digital registration, in order to distinguish it from other fragments which remain of Pleyte's autopsy.

Unfortunately, no written report was made of the 1990 restoration. It can still be seen that the mask must originally have formed a separate element, as the only part which curved around the body at the rear.[97] The collar, abdomen, legs and feet, on the other hand, seem to have been made in one single piece, although there now are transverse cracks at certain vulnerable areas. The falcon heads of the collar now overlap with the front lappets of the wig, to which they are fixed; originally, the two elements must have been detached of each other. The lateral edges of the body part each terminate along a straight line and are accompanied by a wide framing band of triglyphs and rosettes (Fig. 16). According to the *Aanmerkingen* by Leemans,[98] the sheath would once have continued over the back of the mummy, where according to him it had been closed by a lace originally. However, this is doubtless erroneous, because cartonnages laced at the back rather belong to the Third Intermediate Period.[99] The decoration of Djedhor's cartonnage rather indicates a much later date. We shall see that there exist a number of parallels for this specific type, which suggest that in fact it covered the front and sides of the mummy only.[100] There never was a separately-made rear part to this cartonnage.

Remarkable are the two rows of eight trapezium-shaped or square openings cut *à-jour* in the upper abdomen, with two rows of six narrower slits underneath. These mark the outlines for a number of text columns or figures of deities in the layout of the cartonnage. On the reverse (or inside face) of the surviving sheath the ancient linen shows rectangular patterns in black ink, probably a sketch for the layout of the painted motifs on the front, made in preparation for the cut-out slits and squares.

---

97 Cf. Mekis 2019, 287 with n. 131.

98 See below, *Appendix 1*, p. 2, note *e*.

99 Cf. J.H. Taylor, in: Strudwick/Taylor 2003, 104.

100 For a previous study of Djedhor's cartonnage and its parallels, see Raven 2024. For an earlier note on this type of cartonnages, see already Hellinckx 2002, 210–211.

Fig. 13. Cartonnage of Djedhor, front (RMO, inv. L.XII.2-d).

Basically, the decoration described by Pleyte is still recognizable. The tripartite wig of the mask is painted dark blue, with a concentric fillet around the brow consisting of a text band framed between two friezes of polychrome rectangles and petals. The visible signs were duely copied by Pleyte, and give the text of Book of the Dead spell 151a.[101] This text concerns an identification of the various parts of the face with specific gods, and was a favourite for similar headbands.[102] A winged scarab in yellow and black covers the top of the skull, with a gilt disk held in its front legs and the rear legs terminating in crowned serpents.[103] The rear lappet and its painted motif described by Pleyte is now completely missing. The face and throat of the mask were gilt, as can still be seen from a small fragment remaining on the latter area; otherwise the whole face is now covered in modern linen. There are 9 horizontal rows of a necklace between the front lappets of the wig, and 12 curved ranges of similar petals, rosettes, triglyphs, and diabolo patterns on the collar below. Between necklace and collar is a small gilt *ba* bird on a blue ground. The collar terminates in two falcon's heads on the shoulders and comprises a lower row of large pendant lotus flowers and buds. A gilt pectoral with squatting Osiris, Isis, and Nephthys covers the centre of the collar.

The area below the collar has the following horizontal registers from top to bottom, all separated by single framing bands of petals, triglyphs and diabolos, rosettes, rectangles, etc.:

(1) a creature (scarab?) with outspread wings in green and black, now largely lost, with the upper row of cut-out squares above (according to Pleyte there were columns of hieroglyphs in between);

(2) a squatting Nut in a red dress with outspread wings in green and black, with the lower row of square openings above providing the outlines for her head and for several short columns of hieroglyphs, now illegible;

(3) a central mummy bier flanked by the adoring figures of Isis and Nephthys standing behind serpents on pedestals, all in gold on dark blue, with to the far left and right two Sons of Horus each on red or green grounds (slits outlining the Sons of Horus and the goddesses, short hieroglyphic captions);

(4) two Osiris figures in gold on green, standing back to back to either side of a floral column, and flanked by Isis and Nephthys, Horus and Thoth, the latter presenting the *wedjat* eye (slits again between the areas with gods and goddesses).

101 For the text, cf. Allen 1974, 147–148; Lüscher 1998.

102 Cf. Lüscher 1998, 52–54; Hellinckx 2002, 208–211 with Table CC (including a reference to Djedhor's cartonnage); Mekis 2012, 253; Mekis 2019, 287–288.

103 For the association of the head of the mummy and the scarab, see Hellinckx 2002, 202–203.

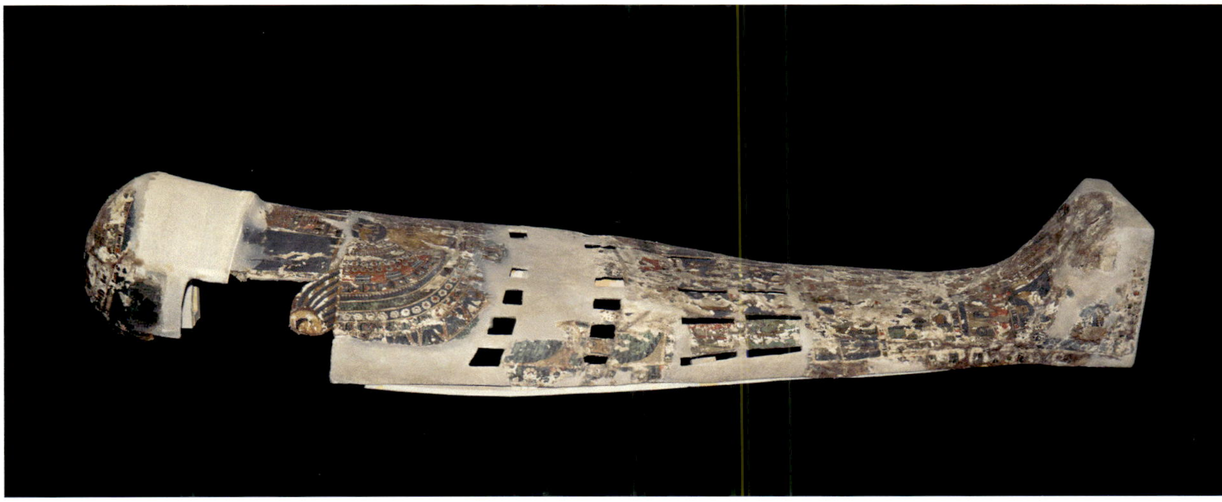

Fig. 14. Cartonnage of Djedhor, side (RMO, inv. L.XII.2-d).

Fig. 15. Cartonnage of Djedhor, detail of upper half (RMO, inv. L.XII.2-c).

Fig. 16. Detail of triglyph-and-rosette frieze along the lateral edges of the cartonnage (RMO, inv. L.XII.2-d).

Then comes a central text column running down to the feet, in black on gold between block friezes, flanked by:

(5) register with two antithetic groups of three standing genii;
(6) ditto register, likewise with two antithetic groups of three standing genii;
(7) two symmetrical groups of four squatting gods in red garments;
(8) two gilt falcons on 'gold' signs on the sides of the feet, with wings extended forwards and each protecting the cartouche of Osiris;
(9) two recumbent black jackals with captions mentioning Wepwawet of the north and south, likewise on the sides of the feet.

Nothing can be seen now of the three-headed serpent mentioned by Pleyte. On the other hand, the Asiatic captives on the soles of the feet and their captions are still there.

7.2. Parallels

Mummy-sheaths restricted to the front, sides and feet, often with a separate mask (though in others it is integrated with the rest of the cover) are a well-known type at Thebes during the Ptolemaic Period.[104] The following close parallels can be mentioned for Djedhor's cartonnage. The most important parallels for our research are of course the cartonnages that still contain a mummy, or are at least associated with one; these burials have been marked with an asterisk (*) and will be often mentioned as parallels in the following chapters. Most cartonnages display a similar decoration with numerous, relatively small figures on a green, blue, or red ground, a *ba*-bird on the chest, a collar with an outer row of lotus flowers, the usual scene of the mummy on the bier, and a strip of inscriptions over the legs. The lateral edges again have edge bands of painted rosettes, the feet have falcons with wings extended forwards, and there are Asiatic captives on the soles of the feet:[105]

- Avignon, Musée Calvet, A 67A. Fragment of the leg section, depicting two registers of *djed* and *tyet* amulets and squatting gods, inscribed for the sistrum-player of Amun-Re Nehemsyrattawy, daughter of the priest Pawerem and the priestess Nestanetjeretten.[106]
- Cairo, Egyptian Museum, JE 25813. Cartonnage of a man Pasheryheby.[107]
- Cortona, Museo dell'Accademia Etrusca. Fragment of chest and right shoulder with part of collar and friezes

104 Cf. Ikram/Dodson 1998, 187, mentioning the tendency for separate cartonnage pieces to join together in the course of the Ptolemaic Period, resulting in a single sheet over the front of the mummy. See also Schreiber 2006; Mekis 2011; Mekis 2012, 249–250; Mekis 2019, 259; Birk 2020, 133–134; Mekis, in: Wagner 2024, 257.

105 For the latter motif, cf. Corcoran 1995, pls. 9, 24, 29; Mekis 2019, 289-290; Elias/Mekis 2019, 160 n. 168. It should be noted that a rosette- and triglyph frieze also occurs around the cartonnage mummy boot of Tarepyt, Cairo TR 21.11.16.13; see Elias/Mekis 2019, Fig. 5f-1.

106 Foissy-Aufrère/Aufrère/Loury 1985, 96–99, § 191–192; J.-C. Goyon, in: Cavalier 2011, 68, Cat. 19; cf. Mekis 2011, 44 Doc. 7.

107 Wagner 2024, 257 n. 1075 with Abb. 29, 31 and 33. I wish to thank T. Mekis for this reference.

of divinities, also along the lateral border (instead of the usual rosettes).[108]

- Derby Museum and Art Gallery, inv. 1872.1. Cartonnage of a man Pashery... (?). Mask as a separate piece.[109]
- * Florence, Museo Archeologico, 5703 B of Takerheb, daughter of the royal scribe and priest Aapehty and the housewife Nebetdenehyt.[110] No cut-out sections, mask made as a separate piece, lavish use of gilding.
- Leipzig, Grassi Museum für Angewandte Kunst, 1906.429, anonymous.[111] Fragment of abdominal section, probably made for a child, and consisting of two registers separated by a band of rosettes, the upper with the mummy on a bier, the lower with Osiris and Horakhte standing back to back, both flanked by protective gods on brightly coloured panels. No cut-out sections, no inscriptions. Estate of Hedwig von Eberstein 1906.
- * London, British Museum, EA 6679 of the god's father and high-priest of Amun in Karnak, Hornedjitef, son of Nekhthorheb and the sistrum-player of Amun, Taditneferhotep (Fig. 17).[112] No cut-out sections, separate mask.
- * London, British Museum, EA 6680 of Horemheb, the son of Padiamunnebnesuttawy and the housewife Pesdet.[113] This cartonnage has cut-out sections just like Djedhor's, with a separate mask.
- Paisley, Paisley Museum, EG 203, 212, and 239.[114] Three fragments of a cartonnage of the god's father Paiuhor, the son of Hor and Taykhybiat. Parts of mask, collar, and soles of feet; mask presumably separately made.
- Paris, Louvre, AF 12859 of the sistrum-player Nestanetjeretten, the daughter of Iahmes and Taukesh.[115] Mask made separately, then fixed to rest of cartonnage, no cut-out sections.
- Rennes, Musée des Beaux-Arts, inv. 873.5.6. Fragment of chest, anonymous, with part of two registers, the upper with a solar barque, the lower with four rectangular sections depicting an offering scene. Legacy by A. Pointeau in 1873, found 1848.[116]
- * Stockholm, Världskulturmuseerna (former Medelhavsmuseet), E.5 of the Montu priest Neswaiu, the son of Tjaimu and Takerheb (Fig. 18). This cartonnage has openwork designs and many gilt details. The mask was made separately.[117]
- Thebes, excavations of TT 32: various fragments (reg. nos. 2000.Ca.001, 2005.Ca.020–021), Nesmin family.[118]
- Thebes, excavations of TT 36: various fragments, Hornedjitef family.[119]
- Thebes, excavations of TT 157: cartonnage of the high-priest of Amun-Re Ankhefenkhonsu, the son of Nesmin and Tashery. Mask probably separately made.[120]
- Turin, Museo Egizio, C. 2257.[121] Cartonnage of a man Imhotep, mother's name illegible. The mask was made separately.
- Turin, Museo Egizio, C. 2258 of Djehutir(di)s son of Tasherytaapehty.[122] Mask integrated with rest of sheath, no openwork designs.
- Warsaw, National Museum, 236805 of Hor-Djehuty. [123]
- Several minor fragments in other collections.[124]

It may be seen that real one-piece cartonnages are rare; they alternate with two-piece items which have a separate mask. Stylistically, both subtypes are very similar with their large *wesekh* collars covering the chest, and underneath numerous registers of relatively small figures on a green, blue, or red ground. Frequently occurring motifs are a *ba*-bird on the chest, a vignette of the mummy on its bier on the abdomen, and a central framed column of inscription over the legs. Very characteristic are the edge bands of painted rosettes, whereas there are usually falcons with their wings extended forwards on the sides of the feet and Asiatic captives under the soles. Thus there is a mixture of traditions deriving from previous periods of coffin design: whereas the large collars and central strips of inscription were established on the yellow coffins of the Third Intermediate Period, vignettes such as the mummy on its bier rather follow Late

108 M.C. Guidotti, in: Bruschetti 1996, 60 with fig. 134 (I wish to thank N. Strudwick for sending me a copy of this publication); cf. Schreiber 2006, 236 n. 43.

109 Unpublished, communication by J.H. Taylor.

110 Guidotti 2001, 6 and 40–41; Guidotti 2003; Guidotti 2009. See also www.globalegyptianmuseum.org *sub* Florence 5708 (*sic!* accessed 25-4-2022). Already mentioned as a parallel by Leemans in his *Aanmerkingen*: see below, *Appendix* 1, p. 3.

111 Personal inspection 2019. I thank Ms. M. Heckhoff of the Grassi Museum for further information.

112 See Dawson/Gray 1968, cat. 48 and pl. XIII; Walker/Bierbrier 1997, 30; J.H. Taylor, in: Dawson/Strudwick 2016, 69 with fig. 44. For this burial ensemble, cf. PM I.2, 623–624; Quaegebeur 1995, 142–144; Strudwick 2006, 294–297.

113 Dawson/Gray 1968, cat. 44 and pl. XII. Cf. PM I.2, 829.

114 Mekis 2012, 251–253 and 267–269; Mekis 2019, 287–290.

115 Mekis 2011, 57–60; Mekis 2012.

116 Rannou 1999, 104, no. 141; cf. Schreiber 2006, 236 n. 43.

117 Lieblein 1868, 14–15, cat. 5; Schmidt 1919, 225 fig. 1300; anonymous 1961, 114 cat. 167; van Hoeij 1998, 36–38. Cf. PM I.2, 832.

118 Schreiber 2006, 228–229, 236 n. 43 (here Schreiber also mentions a fragment from TT 373, which is less convincing); Mekis 2011, 59 n. 50; G. Schreiber, in: Bács *et al.* 2009, 122 with n. 10.

119 Wagner 2024, 256ff. with pls. 55–57; I owe this reference to T. Mekis.

120 Mekis 2011, 58 n. 49.

121 See https://collezioni.museoegizio.it (accessed 25-4-2022). I thank T. Mekis for the reading of the name.

122 Donadoni-Roveri 1988, 232 no. 321; cf. Fabretti/Rossi/Lanzone 1882, 320–321. Cf. also Mekis 2019, 259 n. 12. Mother's name as read by T. Mekis (personal communication).

123 Communication by T. Mekis; see Wagner 2024, 257 n. 1076 with Abb. 28 and 32.

124 T. Mekis, in: Wagner 2024, 257, n. 1974.

Fig. 17. Cartonnage of Hornedjitef (London, British Museum EA 6679. Image CC BY-NC-SA 4.0, © The Trustees of the British Museum).

Fig. 18. Cartonnage of Neswaiu (Stockholm, Världskulturmuseerna E.5. Photo by Ove Kaneberg, Världskulturmuseerna. By kind permission of Sofia Häggman).

Period examples.[125] The cut-out slits rather remind one of the openwork mummy covers of bent wood dating to the Ramesside Period.[126] Such covers (also known as 'mummy boards') have other features in common with the Ptolemaic single-sheet or two-part cartonnages: they likewise covered only the front part of the body, and they came with masks which were either detached or integrated with the rest of the cover. Therefore, the Ptolemaic mummy sheaths are characteristic of the eclectic tastes of the period.

The fact that four of these cartonnages still have their mummies is particularly interesting for our research. Whereas the Leiden mummy of Djedhor was dissected by Pleyte in 1878, the Florence specimen of Takerheb was partially unwrapped as early as 1827 by Rosellini and Migliarini.[127] Some details on the British Museum mummies of Hornedjitef and Horemheb can be found in Dawson's publication of the X-ray research done by Gray,[128] and in a publication following recent scans of Hornedjitef's mummy.[129] The Stockholm mummy of Neswaiu was recently scanned by computer tomography, and a museum display of the results was prepared by the Swedish firm of Interspectral; several impressions of this investigation can be found on the internet.[130] All this helps to interpret the information given by Pleyte in his detailed report of the 1878 autopsy. Of course, an autopsy provides a different kind of information than an X-ray or a mummy CT-scan. Therefore, it is fortunate that we are now able to compare the results of both types of investigations. These parallels shed an interesting light on the archaeological context and social background of Djedhor. We shall have occasion to refer to various aspects of these comparative burials in the following chapters. Finally, in Chapter 18 below on Djedhor's social status we shall speculate on the nature of these comparisons.

125 Cf. already Schreiber 2006, 231–233.

126 See Cooney 2007, 22–28, 197–199.

127 Birch 1855.

128 Dawson/Gray 1968.

129 Filer 1999.

130 www.bbc.com/news/technology-26664927; www.youtube.com/watch?v=u5ncNCH4MNc; www.youtube.com/watch?v=kXaeJQR-CkM; www.youtube.com/watch?v=URo4MSZLurs.

Chapter 8

The garlands

8.1. Pleyte as an amateur-botanist

The first forty lines of the *procès-verbal* present a report on the acquisition and original registration and description of the burial ensemble. This introduction states that Reuvens was the first to collect some of the loose elements of the Djedhor mummy. These included the remains of one or more leaf garlands, which had been carefully investigated and conserved by Pleyte already in 1877, the year before his autopsy of Djedhor's mummy.

Here one should realise that Willem Pleyte was one of the first Egyptologists to take a keen interest in botanical matters.[131] His first recorded endeavour to explore this hitherto neglected aspect of Ancient Egyptian culture consists of a written notice on the Egyptian acacia tree, compiled for the new dictionary of the Dutch language by M. de Vries and L.A. te Winkel and dated to 1866.[132] Ten years later, Pleyte presented a communication dealing with the Egyptian lotus, on the occasion of the annual meeting of the Dutch Botanical Society. This was published in the acts of the meeting in question.[133]

In the light of this interest, it is not surprising that Pleyte started a search for Ancient Egyptian botanical remains present in the Leiden collections. This may have been instigated by the Berlin botanist Paul Ascherson, who visited the Leiden Museum in 1877 and was one of Pleyte's correspondents.[134] In the framework of this visit Pleyte studied various funerary garlands still extant on the mummies of the Late Period Theban priest Ankhhor (inv.no. RO.III-e) and of a boy dating to the Roman Period (inv.no. AMM 24-a).[135] The two men also investigated the remains of several other garlands, previously removed from various mummies of the collection and then deposited in a box and two saucers kept in the museum's reserves.[136] All these leaves and flowers were properly identified by Ascherson and then carefully mounted between sheets of glass by Pleyte.

The box and the two saucers are also mentioned on a document kept in the RMO Archives, copied from Pleyte's original notes and signed by Leemans, dated 6 July 1877.[137] This report of the research by Pleyte and Ascherson makes clear that it was sometimes

131 For the following, see already Raven 1993, 71; Greco/Oeters/Raven 2012, 75–78; Raven, in: Ter Keurs/Wirtz 2018, 170–173.

132 Mentioned by Hasselbach 1987, 95.

133 Pleyte 1876.

134 See various letters by Ascherson in the RMO Archives, 19.7.2/1: Archives Pleyte, Correspondence. Cf. also Pleyte 1882, 43. For Ascherson, see https://nl.wikipedia.org/wiki/Paul_Friedrich_August_Ascherson.

135 Cf. Raven/Taconis 2005, cat. 16 and 30, respectively.

136 In his *Aanmerkingen* (below, Appendix 1, p. 1 n. *e*), Leemans states: 'The loose bandages or wrappings with inscriptions had been deposited by Reuvens in a wooden box, closed by means of a sheet of glass glued on top.'

137 RMO Archives, 6.4.3/18 *sub* 9 (box C98). The Djedhor garlands are mentioned under no. 4. For illustrations of other garlands from the same report, see Raven 1993, fig. 101; Greco/Oeters/Raven 2012, Fig. 22; Raven, in: Ter Keurs/Wirtz 2018, 171 fig. 2.

Fig. 19. Garland as framed by Pleyte (RMO, inv. Am 10-b).

difficult to properly connect the decayed garlands with their original mummies. Especially the box seems to have contained a mixture of various items.[138] For the saucers the situation was slightly better, since one of them was provided with a label in the handwriting of Reuvens, referring to the *Mumia Lescluziana 1824* (i.e. the mummy dissected in that year together with Van Breda and Sandifort)[139], the other was labelled *Mumia Lescluziana ex auctione 1826 ... Cap XII.no. 2* and thereby clearly contained material deriving from Djedhor's mummy. All remains of leaves and flowers were entered in the museum's registers in the same year under inv.nos. Am 1–18. Three years later, Pleyte presented his findings, again in an annual meeting of the Dutch Botanical Society.[140]

138 Mentioned by Pleyte as a box full of leaves and flowers (page 2 of the document mentioned in the previous footnote). See also Leemans 1840, 85, Cat. H 41.

139 *Supra*, § 2.1.

140 Pleyte 1882.

8.2. Djedhor's mummy garlands

Thanks to this meticulous research, Pleyte was already able to state in the *procès-verbal* of his 1878 autopsy (*sub* 46b) that the Djedhor mummy originally had one garland on the head and another on the chest. These were said to consist of the leaves of *Mimusops kummel*, strung on cords of *doum* palm fibres (*Hyphaene thebaica*). The inventory numbers given there (Am 11–13) are not correct. According to the 1877 inventory book, Am 10 is one of Djedhor's garlands (Am 10-b in the new digital registration, in order to distinguish it from other objects), and Am 11 (Am 11-c digital registration) consists of the remains of several palm fibre strings from the same mummy (Figs. 19–20).[141] The whereabouts of the other garland purported to belong with Djedhor's mummy cannot be ascertained, but a few remains are kept in the reserves under no. L.XII.2-g.

141 Inventaris RMO no. 10, page 83.

Fig. 20. Palm-fibre cords of garlands (RMO, inv. Am 11-c).

Already in his presentation for the Botanical Society of 1882, Pleyte put the question why the Egyptians would have deposited this kind of flower garlands on the mummies of their deceased relatives. Two years later, he himself provided an answer to this question, in a communication for the International Congress of Orientalists held in Leiden in 1884.[142] Here he dealt with the religious significance of such leaf garlands, connecting them with Chapters 19 and 20 of the Book of the Dead. Both are entitled 'spell for wreaths of vindication', whereas Chapter 19 explicitly states it has to be 'uttered over wreaths put on a man's head'.[143] These ritual texts do not specify which flowers or leaves had to be selected for this purpose. Clearly, the garlands may be considered to represent a symbol of victory, given to those deceased who succesfully left the hall of justice after the Judgment of the Dead (involving the weighing of the heart). It is characteristic of Egyptian magic that the (rather premature) gift of such a garland already during the burial was regarded as an effective guarantee for the positive outcome of the Judgment, even though the latter had not yet taken place at the moment of interment.

Neither publication refers to the Djedhor garlands in any detail, but several parallels are mentioned for the custom to deposit a garland of leaves and flowers around the head of a mummy. According to Pleyte the use of *mimusops* leaves (also known as persea) alternates with those of the olive, and the similarity of the leaves of both species to the laurel may explain their use for garlands in the Ptolemaic Period. Pleyte's remark seems to hint at influence of the Greek culture, where the use of laurel garlands had a long tradition.[144] In the case of Djedhor, who lived during the Ptolemaic Period (although Pleyte was still convinced he had to be dated to Dynasty XXV–XXVI)[145] such a derivation would of course not be impossible, although funerary ritual in a provincial place like Thebes was on the whole very traditional and rather immune to influence from the culture of the European conquerers.

However, we do not need Greek influence to explain the use of leaf garlands in Egyptian burial rituals, as is proved by the above-mentioned texts from the Book of the Dead. Olive garlands had already been given to the dead from at least Dynasty XVIII onwards, long before the conquest by Alexander, as is shown by several wreaths from the tomb of Tutankhamun.[146] Olive leaves were also found on Ankhhor's mummy in the RMO, whereas persea was preferred for the Roman Period mummy investigated by Pleyte at the same time.[147] Though Germer remarks that in the Ptolemaic Period the persea seems to have become rare, this circumstance does not seem to have put an end to the use of its leaves in contemporary funerary garlands.[148] The identification by Pleyte and Ascherson of the leaves of Djedhor's mummy as *Mimusops kummel* cannot be taken at face value, because according to modern research *Mimusops schimperi* was much more common in Ancient Egypt.[149] In this respect it is relevant to point out that a leaf

142 Pleyte 1884.

143 Cf. Allen 1974, 34–36 (Spell 19, P 1 and T 2; Spell 20, P).

144 In Egypt, the laurel tree was probably not indigenous before the Hellenistic period; see Germer1985, 14–15.

145 See his remarks in the *procès-verbal*, page 15.

146 P.E. Newberry, in: Carter 1927, 189–196. Cf. Germer 1985, 150 with n. 3.

147 See the above-mentioned report (RMO Archives, 6.4.3/18 *sub* 9 (box C98)), nos. 1 and 2, respectively.

148 Cf. Germer 1985, 149.

149 *Ibid.*, 148–149.

garland from Neswaiu's mummy (whose cartonnage was recognized as a parallel of Djedhor's in Chapter 7) is still kept in the Världskulturmuseerna in Stockholm under no. A.04.H.04. This has indeed been identified as consisting of leaves of *Mimusops schimperi*,[150] and the same may be true for Djedhor's mummy. The Ptolemaic mummy of Tarepyt in Cairo (TR 21.11.16.13) – which has a 4-piece cartonnage and therefore does not belong to our standard reference set – has numerous leaf garlands crosswise over the body, as well as a 'wreath of vindication' around the brow. The leaves have been provisionally identified as *Mimusops laurifolia*.[151]

150 See collections.smvk.se/carlotta-mhm/web/object/3015853, *sub* Comments. Cf. Laurent-Täckholm 1940.

151 See Elias/Mekis 2019, Figs. 5b-2 and 5e-1.

Chapter 9

The bead net

Fig. 21a. Bead net of unknown burial (Louvre N 3078, © Musée du Louvre, Dist. GrandPalais Rmn / Christian Décamps).

Unfortunately, the beads mentioned in the *procès-verbal* (*sub* 46a) cannot be identified among the present-day collections, suggesting there were only a few of them that may have been mixed up with other material.[152] We have no information on the appearance of the beads concerned, although the majority must have consisted of plain cylinder beads, since according to Pleyte they belonged to a bead net covering the mummy. Doubtless, the net lay on top of the mummy, inside (or underneath) the cartonnage mummy-sheath, but this is not clear from Pleyte's report. Such bead nets were a regular phenomenon on Egyptian mummies from Dynasty XXI onwards, and especially during the Late Period. However, some isolated examples have been dated as late as the Ptolemaic Period.[153]

In fact, there seems to be a closely related group of bead nets, presumably connected with Ptolemaic burials at Thebes and often overlooked during modern research:

- Neswaiu's mummy in Stockholm still has a bead net which extends from chest to ankles.[154]
- A very similar bead net can be found in the Louvre, acquired with the Salt collection in 1826 (inv. N 3078) and wrongly dated to Dynasties 27–30 (Fig. 21a–b).[155]
- A net of the same type was already illustrated by Cailliaud in 1831.[156]
- A net with slightly different design still lies on the Ptolemaic mummy of Tarepyt from Thebes, now in the Egyptian Museum in Cairo (TR 21/11/16/13, SR 4/11354).[157]

These nets cover the mummy from chest to ankles, where they end in a tasseled fringe. All of them have a characteristic patterned band in mosaic work which spans the chest. These chest bands usually have an upper section with a symmetrical composition of a central scarab flanked by *djed* pillars and antithetic jackals on shrines (though Tarepyt has seven *djed* pillars instead). Above and below, this band is framed between various other decorative strips comprising X-shaped motifs or block friezes. Then follows a lower section decorated with zigzag motifs in various colours. This forms the transition to the proper net and its lozenge-shaped cells of cylinder beads, again sometimes in various colours. This openwork part of the net may also be framed above and along the sides by block frieze bands in mosaic work.

Unfortunately, information on the exact provenance and archaeological background of these items is rather scanty. Cailliaud may well have seen his specimen in Thebes during

152 A single broken cylinder bead and a single ring bead, both of blue faience, are included in the plastic bag with the bulb of garlic M47b.19 found on Djedhor's mummy (cf. § 13.2 below).

153 Dawson/Gray 1968, cat. 50 and pl. XIII (EA 20745); Silvano 1980, 83 n. 4; Von Recklinghausen 2007, 216–225 (2nd–1st cent. BC, el-Hibeh); Manley/Dodson 2010, cat. 43.

154 See www.youtube.com/watch?v=URo4MSZLurs.

155 Champollion 2013, 256, cat.no. P.314 with ill. N 3078.

156 Cf. Cailliaud 1831, pl. 22; reproduced in Bresciani 1996, fig. 38.

157 Elias/Mekis 2019, 156 with fig. 5e-1.

Fig. 21b. Detail of chest band, bead net of unknown burial, (Louvre N 3078, © Musée du Louvre, Dist. GrandPalais Rmn / Christian Décamps).

one of his travels, and a Theban provenance of Salt's bead net is also well possible. Therefore, it is rather frustrating that of Djedhor's bead net (certainly of Theban provenance, as we shall see below in Chapter 19) no more than a few loose beads seem to have gone to Leiden. However, it is a tempting possibility to consider that the Louvre net may well have belonged to Djedhor's mummy, since there are more items of his burial which ended up in Paris.[158] Again, Henry Salt may have had a hand in this.[159]

158 See § 16.4 below and Fig. 52.
159 Cf. *infra*, § 19.6.

Chapter 10

Outer wrappings

10.1. Inscribed bandages

Next, Pleyte describes the remains of 93 fragments of linen bandages inscribed with texts, mainly taken from the Book of the Dead. Presumably, most of these bandages were already lying loose when he found them, and accordingly they were labelled under the heading 46c. Most of these fragments can still be found in the Leiden collections, although the count of the exact number of fragments is rather problematic since several of them have been joined together in order to reconstruct the original bandages. In total, there are now four cardboard frames with 9, 10, 7 and 10 bandages, respectively (several of them joined from a number of different fragments). These four frames have been labelled M 46c and are registered as inventory numbers AL 51 vel 1–4 in the modern digital registration (cf. Fig. 22 for one of these frames).[160] Apart from these, there are two modern glass frames with 7 and 6 additional fragments (inv.nos. AL 51 vel 6–7); presumably these had come loose from the original cardboard frames and they do not bear any autopsy labels. There is also a cardboard frame labelled M 47b.1–10 (inventory number AL 51 vel 5), which can be identified as the fragmentary bandages removed by Pleyte himself from the back of the thighs (Fig. 23).[161]

The inscriptions are in single lines of cursive hieroglyphs, or rather bold hieratic, and have been written in black ink. On several bandages one can read the titles and genealogy of Djedhor, as already mentioned by Pleyte, thus proving that the mummy indeed belongs together with the cartonnage. The bandages are 2.2 to 4.0 cm wide and have a maximum length of 140 cm. The old inventory book (used before the modern digital registration) gives numbers AL 51–58 instead, subdivided according to a number of specific spells from the Book of the Dead also mentioned by Pleyte in his autopsy (fragments 71–93), but their exact correlation with the new numbers or the extant fragments is rather unclear. The bandages were also mentioned in a recent catalogue of the pharaonic and Coptic textile collection in Leiden.[162]

According to Pleyte, these bandages formed the mummy's outer wrappings, immediately under the bead net and (partly) under an exterior coating of pitch or bitumen. He thinks there may have been enough to wrap the whole mummy from head to feet, perhaps even in a double layer. These statements can be compared with Migliarini's report on the Florence mummy, which – under a 'wrapper' or mummy shroud covering the exterior and fastened behind – also had an outer layer ('first cement') of resinous or wax-like material (also containing some lime), which had been applied with a brush.[163] Under this layer appeared text bandages similar to those in Leiden, especially concentrated on the legs. Moreover,

---

160 Dutch *vel* = English 'sheet' or 'frame'.
161 Cf. pp. 6–7 of the *procès-verbal.*
162 Van 't Hooft *et al.* 1994, Cat. 355.
163 Birch 1855, 162.

Fig. 22. Bandages with hieratic texts (RMO, inv. AL 51 vel 1).

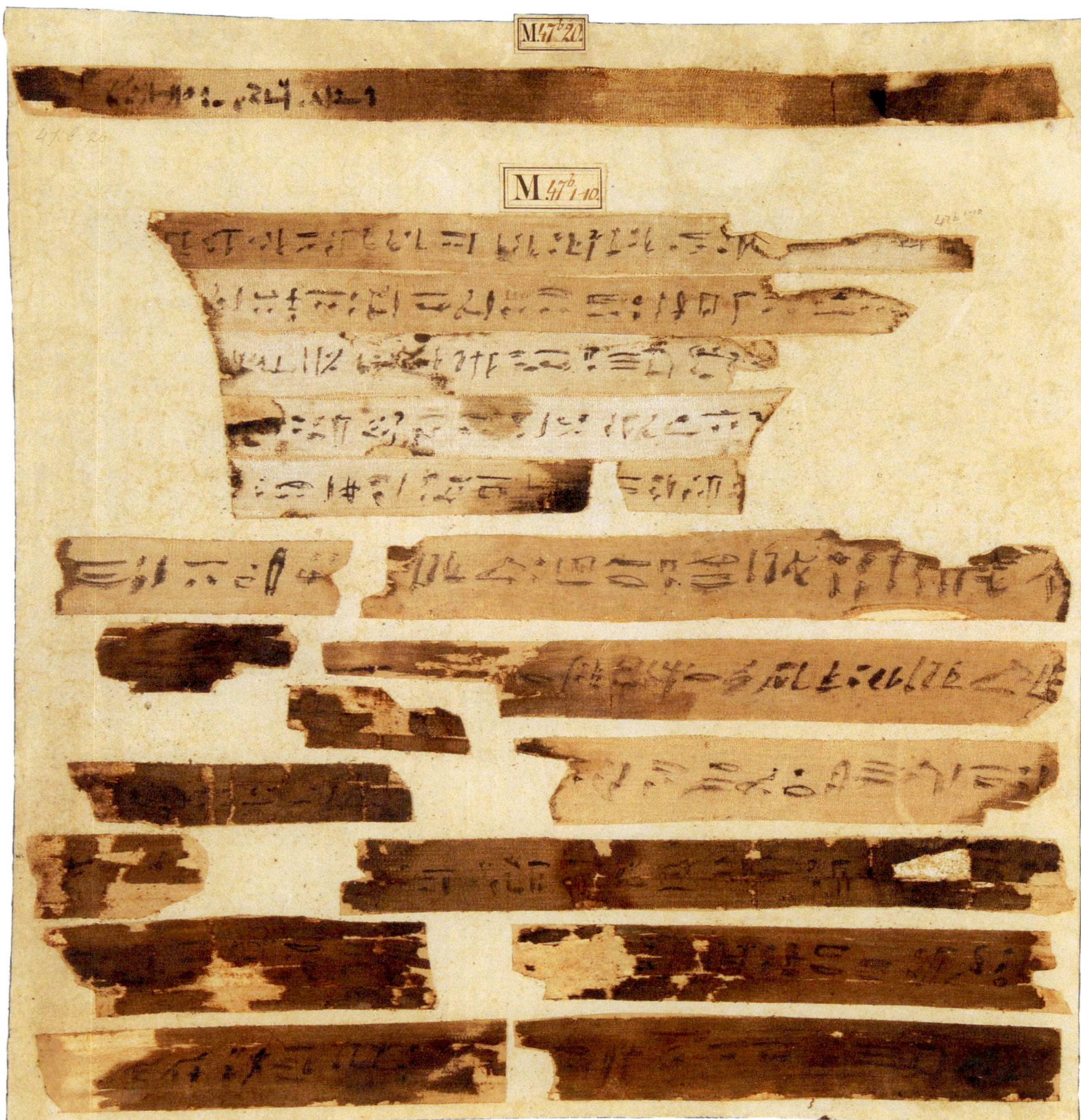

Fig. 23. Bandages with hieratic texts (RMO, inv. AL 51 vel 5).

Fig. 24. Vignettes of twelve deities and a phoenix in a barque on linen (RMO, inv. AL 42–43).

the bandages are described as being subdivided in a right and a left half, each provided with demotic numbers.[164] Although such added position numbers are well known from other inscribed bandages,[165] they are lacking on the Djedhor wrappings. The Florence wrappings are also inscribed with hieratic texts from the Book of the Dead; their length is described as varying from 3.59 to 5.71 m.[166] Some of Takerheb's missing bandages have recently been retrieved in the Canterbury Museum in Christchurch, New Zealand.[167] The practice of inscribing texts from the Book of the Dead on mummy bandages seems to have started during the Late Period. The Djedhor bandages belong to the third class distinguished by De Caluwe: bandages with a single line of hieroglyphs or hieratic and of a restricted width.[168] Such narrow bands with no more than three lines of texts seem to be especially characteristic of the Theban area.[169]

10.2. Fragmentary vignettes

Pleyte then mentions, under number 46d, the remains of small vignettes on linen representing twelve mummiform deities and a barque in which the deceased transfers a phoenix bird. These vignettes in black ink are still kept in the Leiden collection (inv.nos. AL 42–43, Fig. 24).[170] They have been cut out by Pleyte and stuck onto cardboard, so that the original composition and dimensions of the textiles in question cannot be ascertained. The drawing of the barque could be a vignette of spell 100 of the Book of the Dead, the text of which specifies that such a drawing should be placed on the chest of the mummy. Though images of solar barques or Sokaris barques are not uncommon on mummy shrouds, those are of a different type than the vignette of BD 100.[171] The six human-headed and six serpent-headed mummies are not so easy to identify. According to Pleyte they depict the nightly hours, but that is far from clear. Parallels for these vignettes seem to be lacking in the Florence set of Takerheb. However, they bear a remarkable resemblance to a number of vignettes found on linen fragments in TT 32, likewise depicting standing mummiform deities with either human or serpent's heads.[172] These suggest that the twelve deities were originally represented on an equal number of narrow bandages, and have not been cut out by Pleyte from a larger piece of cloth.

10.3. Osiris shroud

Among these loose textile fragments (46d), Pleyte also found parts of a large shroud with a black ink representation of Osiris. This fragment is now kept under inventory number AL 38 and depicts the god in frontal view with the *atef* crown and holding his sceptres (Fig. 25).[173] The figure had presumably already been removed by Reuvens, and was catalogued as no. O 48 by Leemans in 1840.[174] Pleyte also refers to the similarity between the barque with phoenix

164 Birch 1855, 162–163 and pl. XV.B; reproduced in Raven 1993, fig. 95; see also Rosati 2003, 46.

165 E.g. Van 't Hooft *et al.* 1994, Cat. 337, 341, 354. Cf. De Caluwe 1991, xvii with n. 28.

166 Rosati 2003, 47.

167 Guidotti 2009, 25; Rosati 2009, 218. The items were discovered by Tamás Mekis, together with Takerheb's Book of the Dead papyrus and some more textiles.

168 De Caluwe 1991, xviii–xix.

169 De Caluwe 1991, xx; Mosher 2010, 126. For another close parallel to Djedhor's bandages, see Caminos 1982. For more examples, see now Kockelmann 2008.

170 Van 't Hooft *et al.* 1994, Cat. 152.

171 Parlasca 1966, Tf. 1.4, 52.1, 52.3, 57.1–2, 58.1–2; Grimm 1974, Tf. 8.1, 110.4, 111.3, 112.1–5, 115.1 and .3; Bresciani 1996, figs. 5, 10, 14, 19, 21, 32.

172 Schreiber 2007, 339 with n. 11 (referring to the Djedhor fragments in Leiden), 349 figs. 7–14.

173 Van 't Hooft *et al.* 1994, Cat. 149.

174 Leemans 1840, 199, Cat. O 48.

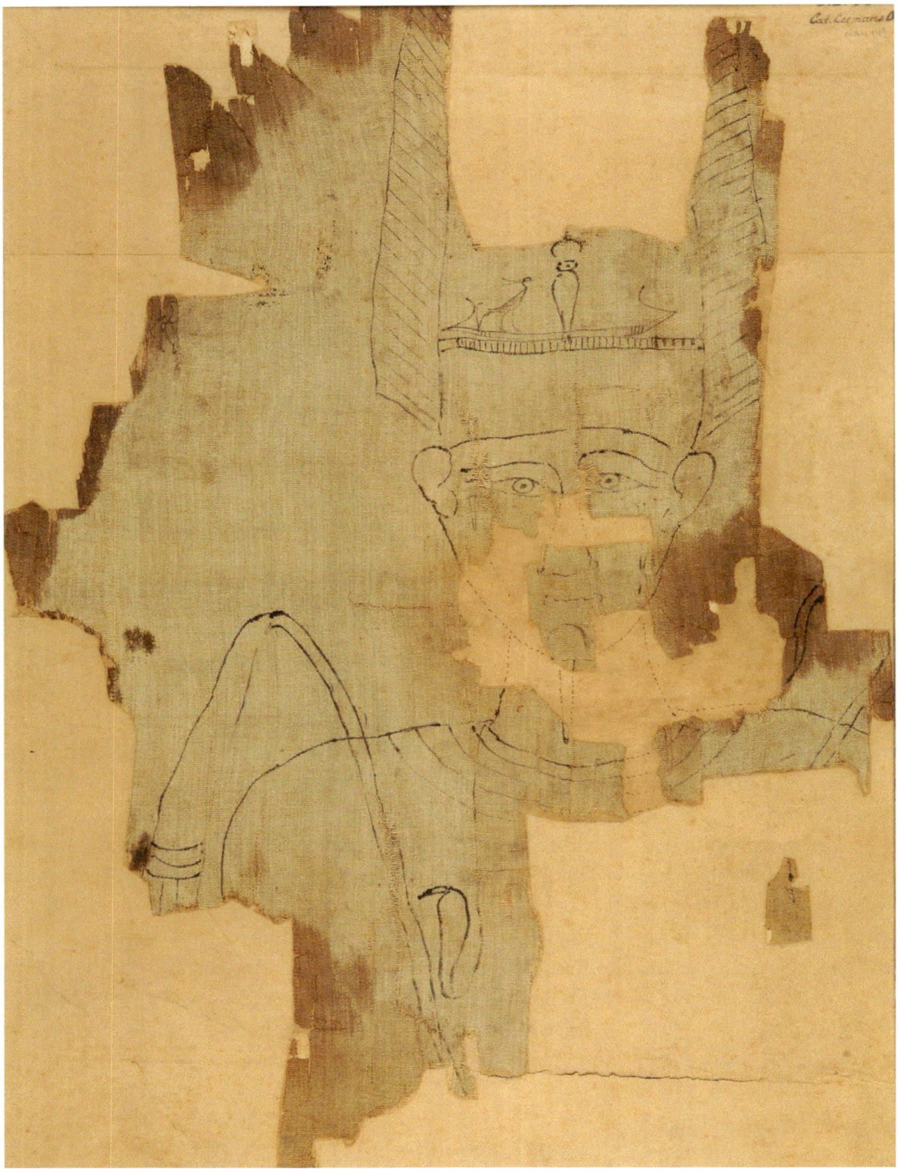

Fig. 25. Fragmentary Osiris shroud (RMO, inv. AL 38).

drawn on the front of the *atef* crown, and the other barque of the loose fragment AL 43 mentioned above.

A similar Osiris figure was found by Migliarini on the Florence mummy,[175] and more parallels have been found in TT 32 in the Theban necropolis.[176] According to Migliarini the Florence shroud served as the cover for a second layer of 'cement' and thereby presented the mummy as Osiris himself. Pleyte also mentions an 'inpenetrable layer of pitch' coming up under the Osiris shroud. His report gives a vivid impression of the hard work it took to break up this layer. Together with the exterior resinous layer and the layer directly adhering to the skin, there may have been three separate layers of resinous material. In fact, three separate layers of densely delineated wrappings (one close to the skin, one on the exterior, and the third at an intermediate level) can be found on several mummies of the Ptolemaic and Roman Periods in Leiden.[177] Three separate layers are also described by Migliarini for the Florence mummy, which had several patterned wrappings between the second and third layers. Due to the hardness of these bituminous layers on Djedhor's mummy, the exact position of the following finds mentioned by Pleyte cannot always be ascertained.

175 Birch 1855, 163. Not found in the present-day collection: Guidotti 2009, 22, 25.

176 Schreiber 2007, 340–341.

177 Raven/Taconis 2005, 163, 167, 173; cf. 178, 182, 188.

Chapter 11

Anklets and sandals

11.1. Anklets

After his remarks about the loose parts of the Djedhor mummy, Pleyte presents the *procès-verbal* of his autopsy of the mummy itself. First of all, he investigated the leg fragment (M 47a). This provided a pair of anklets made of linen covered in stucco, then painted and gilded (autopsy number 47a.1–2). Later on, the torso fragment produced fragments of armlets and wristlets of similar design (47b.17). Altogether, no more than three specimens have been preserved of the six bands once extant (inv.nos. AL 47a–c, Fig. 26). These bands were fastened around the limbs by means of a string at the rear. Anklets of a non-metallic material were also detected by X-raying the mummies of Horemheb and Hornedjitef in the British Museum,[178] whereas Migliarini found actual examples on the mummy of Takerheb in Florence.[179] The simple design in brown (originally red?) and gold is restricted to alternating vertical strokes framed between two circular borders. Doubtless this imitates the common type of anklets worn by the living, and manufactured in rows of beads of various materials and colours strung between metal spacers.[180] Clearly, the present anklets and bracelets are simplified versions of fragile manufacture, especially made for the dead and unsuitable for daily use.

11.2 Sandals

The Florence mummy also provided a parallel for the cartonnage soles bound under the feet, painted with a fine checkered pattern just like Djedhor's specimens (inv. no. AL 46a–b).[181] Such miniature checkered patterns (in imitation of either basketry or beadwork) were a favourite design also on other items of the contemporary burial ensemble, such as cartonnage masks and foot covers.[182] It should be noted that on contemporary or Roman Period mummy shrouds the deceased is often depicted as wearing sandals.[183] Djedhor's soles were fastened under the feet by means of thin string, whereas one of the linen bandages wrapped around the feet bore a black-ink mark in the shape of a sandal (autopsy M47a.3–6).[184] All these elements have been mounted on a single piece of cardboard by Pleyte (Fig. 27).

---

178 Dawson/Gray 1968, 24 (no. 44) and 27 (no. 48).
179 Birch 1855, 167; Guidotti 2009, 25 (inv. 5715–5719). Cf. Elias/Mekis 2019, 152–153 with n. 122.
180 Cf. Andrews 1996, 160–163 with fig. 143.
181 Birch 1855, 167; Guidotti 2009, 23, 25 (inv. 5703, 5705–5706).
182 Cf. e.g. Grimm 1974, pls. 2–4.
183 *Ibid.*, pls. 111.3, 115–118; Bresciani 1996, figs. 14–15, 18–21, 72.
184 Shaped like Gardiner, Sign-list S 33.

Fig. 26. Anklet of cartonnage (RMO, inv. AL 47).

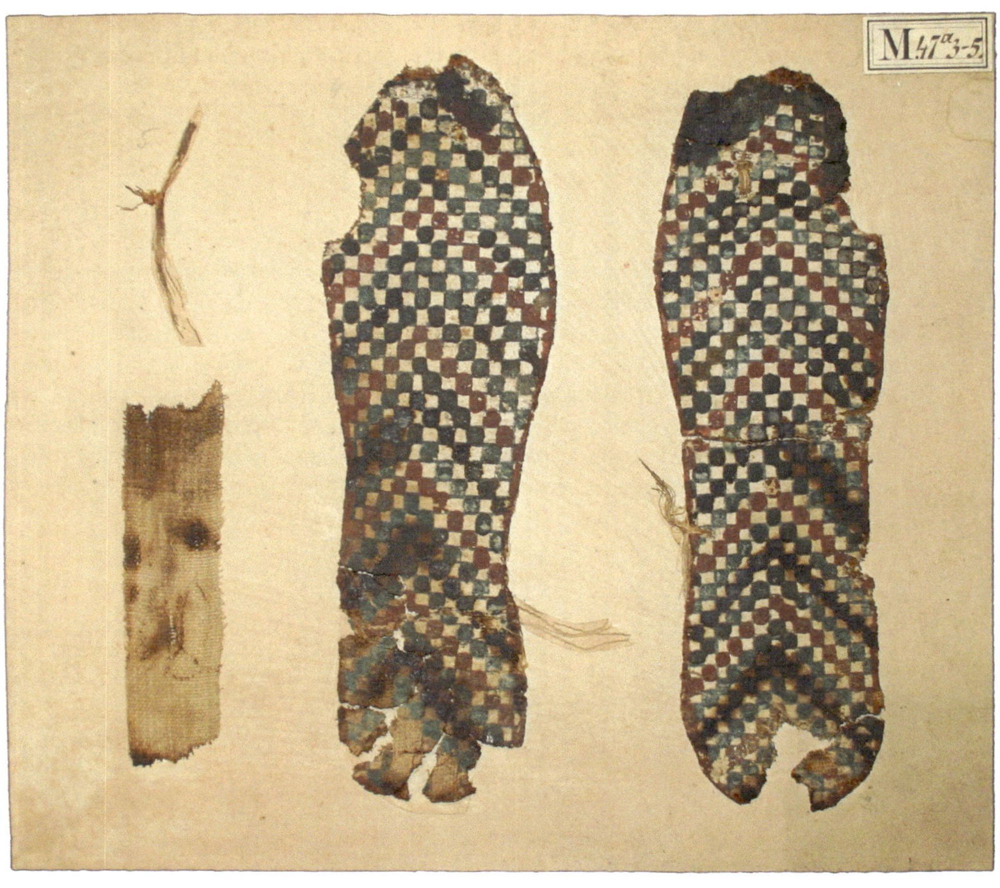

Fig. 27. Footsoles made of cartonnage, remains of string, and bandage with ink mark (RMO, inv. AL 46a–b).

11.3. Gilded nails

Otherwise, the autopsy report mentions that the nails of Djedhor's feet were gilded – as were those of his hands.[185] Several 19th-century scholars imply that this phenomenon was rather common in certain periods.[186] However, there are no more than about seven instances which have been recorded in a reliable manner. Five of these are datable to Dynasty XXX or the Ptolemaic Period. Although Aufrère has asserted that this gilding was itself a cheap substitute for the use of solid gold toe stalls, and therefore a characteristic of cheaper mummies,[187] this conclusion seems to be too rash, since the recorded instances include at least two other mummies which can be regarded as elite burials. As we shall see, Djedhor's own interment likewise betrays that he belonged to the upper echelons of contemporary society.

185 *Supra*, § 5.2, pages 6 and 8, respectively.
186 For the following, see Hellinckx 2002, 20–22 with Table D.
187 Aufrère 1991, II.381.

Chapter 12

The Book of the Dead papyrus

12.1. Find and description

No more finds were made on the leg fragment of Djedhor's mummy. On the other hand, a rich array of objects was retrieved from the torso (fragment M 47b). Pleyte's list starts with nos. 1–10: fragments of narrow linen bandages still adhering to the back of the thighs, which have already been mentioned above in Chapter 10 (see also Fig. 23). Under no. 11, he mentions a rolled-up funerary papyrus which was positioned on the abdomen, roughly from the navel downwards according to the note in the inventory book, where the manuscript was assigned the inv.no. AL 61. In order to extract this manuscript from the mummy, Pleyte had to remove both thigh-bones and part of the abdominal wall, but in spite of this rough treatment the unrolling of the vulnerable papyrus was rather successful. Still, the whole lower edge of the papyrus is now heavily damaged and has crumbled to small fragments. The exterior of the roll, with the text and vignettes of the beginning of the manuscript, was still firmly adhering to the underlying layer of bitumen and had indeed to be sawn out by Pleyte. Thus, the first spells of the Book of the Dead papyrus have suffered a lot.

Today, the manuscript consists of 28 sheets or frames of maximum 39 cm high. These can be compared with the 44 columns listed by Pleyte in his *procès-verbal*. At an unknown moment during the 20th century, these were framed in glass to form 17 sheets altogether (AL 61 vel 1–17) which produce a total length of about 810 cm. Apart from these more or less complete sheets, there are now 6 smaller glass frames holding minor papyrus fragments (AL 61 vel 20 with two pieces, AL 61 vel 21–24 and 28 with numerous small fragments). It is not absolutely certain that all of these belong to the Djedhor manuscript, although most of them have presumably broken off from the lower margins. Apart from these, there are various parts together forming the beginning of the manuscript: one narrow column of full height (AL 61 vel 18) and three frames with smaller fragments (AL 61 vel 25–27), all still caked in bitumen, plus a cardboard folder holding several papyrus fragments of the same initial spells (AL 61 vel 19).

A quick comparison with Pleyte's list gives the following provisional result (see Table 2). It stands to reason that the exact contents of all these chapters ought to be checked critically by a specialist of these texts, since Pleyte did not study the manuscript in great detail. Most spells are accompanied by vignettes in black ink, with some details in red and yellow. The text is in hieratic (Fig. 28), written in black ink with the titles in red, and includes some hieroglyphic captions to the vignettes of spells 125 and 148 (Fig. 29). These confirm the name of the owner as Djedhor, the son of Neferibre and Takerheb, and thereby prove that indeed the papyrus, the mummy cartonnage, and the mummy with its inscribed bandages belong together. The family dossier was first published by Coenen,[188] but the papyrus

188 Coenen 1999, 75.

Inventory number	*Pleyte*	*BD Chapters*
AL 61 vel 18–19, 25–27	Column I	BD 1–4
AL 61 vel 1	Columns II–III	BD 5–12, 14–16
AL 61 vel 2	Columns IV–V	BD 18
AL 61 vel 3	Columns VI–VII	BD 18, 21–24, 30–32
AL 61 vel 4	Columns VIII–IX	BD 33–36, 38–39, 41–42, 44–46
AL 61 vel 5	Columns X–XII	BD 47–51, ?, 110
AL 61 vel 6	Columns XII–XIV	BD 110–111, 113–114, 117–122
AL 61 vel 7	Column XV	BD 125
AL 61 vel 8	Columns XVI–XVII	BD 125, 127–128
AL 61 vel 9	Columns XVIII–XIX	BD 129–132, 137–138
AL 61 vel 10	Columns XX–XXV	BD 145
AL 61 vel 11	Columns XXVI–XXVII	BD 148
AL 61 vel 12	Columns XXVIII–XXXIV	BD 140–142
AL 61 vel 13	Columns XXXV–XXXVI	BD 142, 150, 149
AL 61 vel 14	Columns XXXVI–XXXIX	BD 149, 143, 152, 144
AL 61 vel 15	Columns XXXIX–XLI	BD 144, 151–152, ?
AL 61 vel 16	Column XLII	BD 145, 144
AL 61 vel 17	Columns XLIII–XLIV	BD 161–162

Fig. 28 (opposite page). Sheet from the Book of the Dead papyrus (RMO, inv. AL 61 vel 6).

Fig. 29 (opposite page). Sheet from the Book of the Dead papyrus (RMO, inv. AL 61 vel 11).

Table 2. Layout of the Book of the Dead papyrus of Djedhor.

itself has never been studied in detail. In spite of Pleyte's theories, the Ptolemaic date of the manuscript is beyond all doubt.

12.2. Style and parallels

Regarding the layout of the Djedhor manuscript, this can be seen to conform with Ptolemaic traditions, such as they were studied for instance by Mosher.[189] Thus it may said to belong to his Style 1, with the text being presented continuously in columns of varying widths and without formal borders. The vignettes in black line-drawings have been placed directly beside the titles of the spells wherever they occur in the columns.[190] For spells like BD 145 the vignettes have been arranged in a continuous strip along the top of the page.[191] Some vignettes show details in red, while yellow, white and a greyish hue are also used sparily. The roll reads from right to left, and accordingly the deceased generally faces left – reflecting his onward journey into the realm of the hereafter – whereas the divinities which he meets there face right.[192] Most vignettes have simple register lines only, but those illustrations taking the whole height of the page are properly framed all around. For the human figures and anthropoid divinities, both full-bodied representations and simple stick-figures were used.

189 Mosher 2023.

190 *Ibid.*, 454.

191 Cf. Mosher 2023, 469.

192 *Ibid.*, 454–455.

A similar Book of the Dead manuscript was discovered by Migliarini during the autopsy of the mummy now in Florence.[193] This scroll was likewise placed on the body in a longitudinal position, though not on the abdomen but rather on the chest, under the folded arms.[194] It was fixed in the enveloping layer of bituminous material, just like the Djedhor specimen. Until recently, the whereabouts of this papyrus was unknown, until is was retrieved in the Canterbury Museum in Christchurch (New Zealand), where it has ended up as the result of a 19th-century exchange of objects.[195] This enables us to state its dimensions as long 280 and high 37.3 cm.[196] Thus, it was much shorter than the manuscript of Djedhor. The papyrus was recognized as belonging to a specific Theban type of Book of the Dead manuscripts which often show considerable abridgments.[197] The interment of Hornedjitef likewise contained a Book of the Dead papyrus, of which part is now in the British Museum (EA 10037) and another section in the Pierpont Morgan Library in New York (P. Amherst 35).[198] This

193 Birch 1855, 166.

194 For a papyrus in similar position, see Elias/Mekis 2019, 152 n. 115 with fig. 4c-1.

195 See Rosati 2009. The discovery was made by Tamás Mekis and the papyrus has the inventory numbers EA 1988.73–76.

196 Rosati 2009, 15 n. 13.

197 Mosher 2010, with the Takerheb papyrus being introduced on page 125.

198 Quaegebeur 1995, 142. Cf. Strudwick 2006, 294–296; https://www.britishmuseum.org/research/collection_online/collection_object_details.aspx?objectId=114282&partId=1&museumno=10037 (8 frames).

Fig. 28

Fig. 29

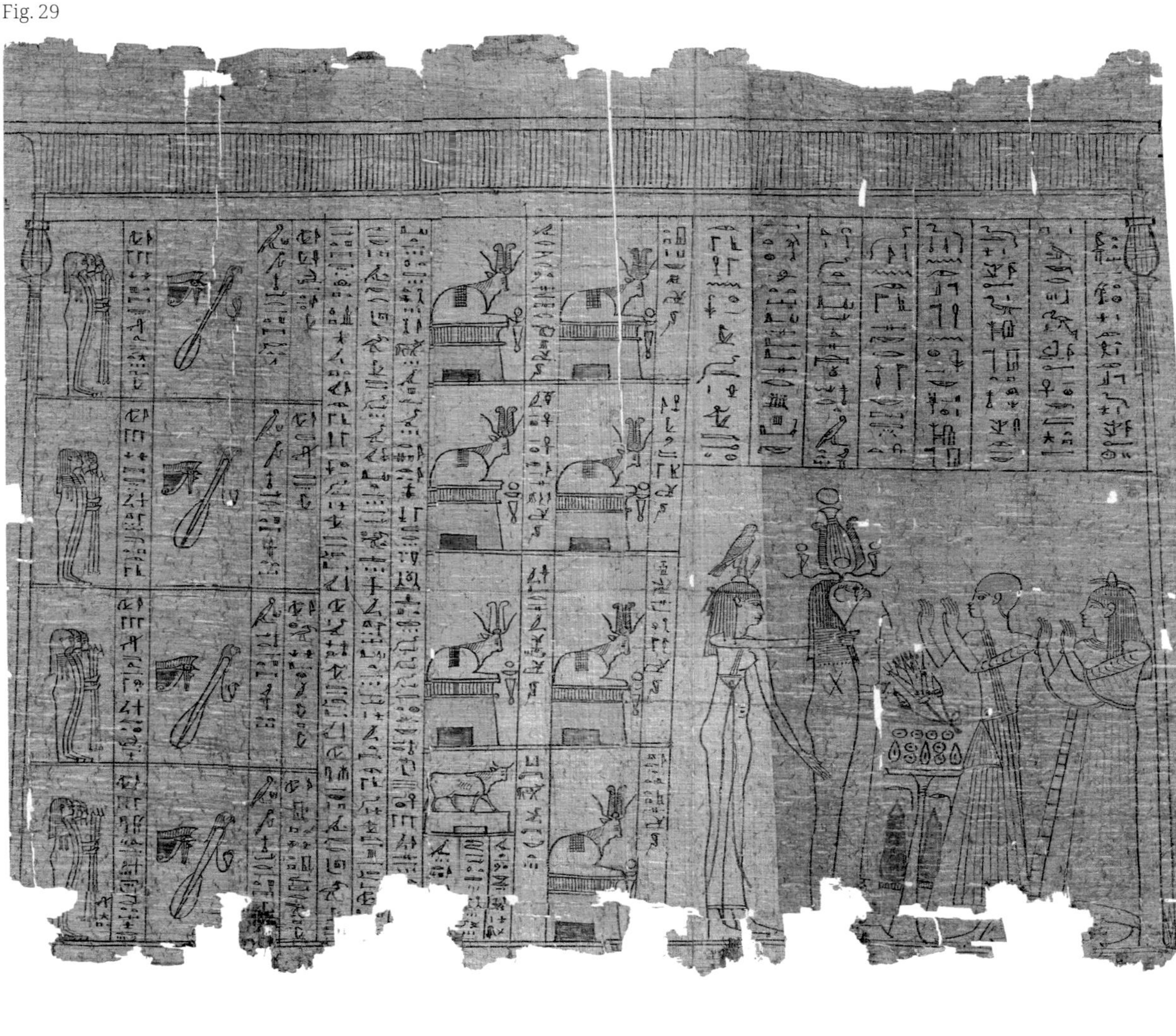

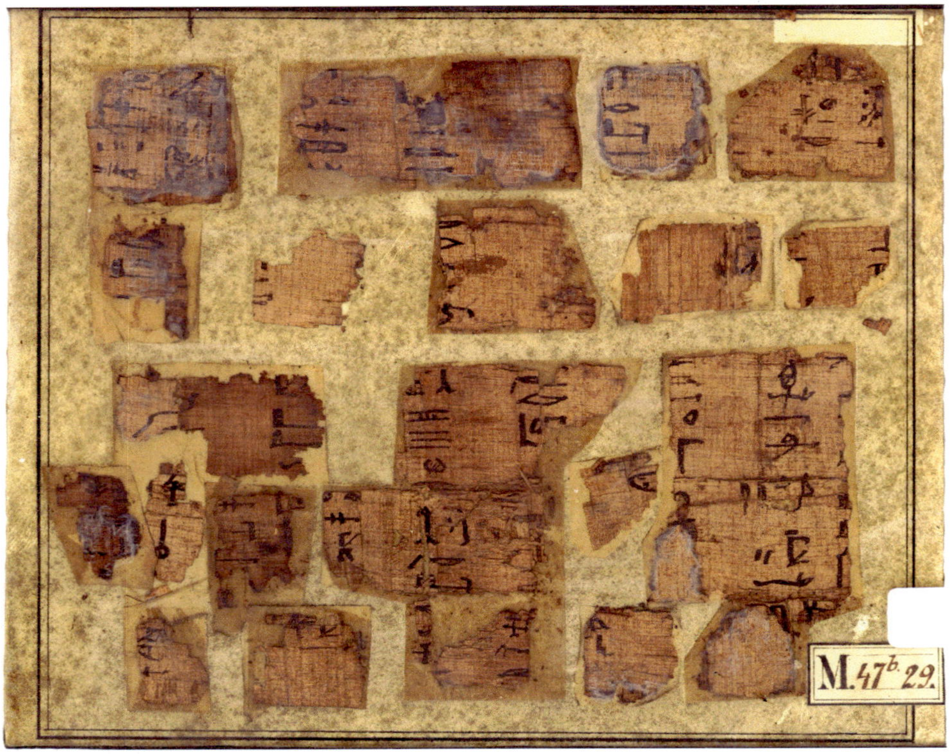

Fig. 30. Remains of small scroll of papyrus (RMO, inv. AL 60).

manuscript was found inside Hornedjitef's inner coffin and is at least 4.5 m long. Other Book of the Dead papyri of our 'reference group' have been preserved for Nestanetjeretten (Vatican 38609),[199] her daughter Nehemsyrattawy (Louvre N 3149 + N 3204 B),[200] and the priest Paiuhor (Munich, Staatliche Bibliothek, Pap.Cod.Hier. 1, 4.a, 4.b).[201] Whether these six papyri belong to the same tradition again needs to be checked in detail by a specialist of these texts. At first sight, at least the vignettes of the various documents look very similar, but this point would reward a further scrutiny.

That Djedhor possessed both a Book of the Dead papyrus and mummy bandages inscribed with various spells from the same corpus appears to be redundant. However, there are various parallels for this apparent reduplication during the Ptolemaic Period. Apart from Takerheb in Florence we may mention the case of the Memphite priest Psamtik, son of Herankh, whose burial can be dated to about 130 BC. His documents were studied by Quirke, who asserts that Psamtik's burial was the only case known containing both a Book of the Dead papyrus and the same texts inscribed on linen bandages.[202] This now proves to be incorrect, as was already stated before by Rosati.[203]

199 Mekis 2011, 66–72.

200 Bellion 1987, 205; Mekis 2011, 44 Doc. 9.

201 Mekis 2012, 263; Mekis 2019, 286-287; Mosher 2019.

202 Quirke 1999, 37.

203 Rosati 2003, 48.

12.3. 'Boarding pass'

A smaller roll of papyrus was found attached to the left side of Djedhor's neck (no. M 47b.29). This was inscribed in black ink in vertical columns of hieroglyphs, comprising at least three columns written next to each other without dividers. The papyrus has fallen apart in small fragments which have been preserved under glass (inv. AL 60, Fig. 30). In spite of its fragmentary state, the text can be recognized as a copy of Book of the Dead chapter 100 (or 129), which was meant to give the deceased a free passage in the solar barque. According to the ritual prescriptions given at the end of this spell, the text had to be said over an image, 'sketched on a clean, unused sheet of papyrus [...] placed on the blessed one's breast without letting it come too close to his body'.[204] Thus, these instructions confirm that this particular chapter of the Book of the Dead had in fact to be written on a separate sheet of papyrus, and was not intended to form part of the larger scroll. Also, it had to be deposited on the chest of the mummy (in Djedhor's case: against the neck) and not to be covered too deep in the wrappings, so that the solar god could easily consult this 'boarding pass'. Even so, Chapter 129 also occurs on sheet 9 of Djedhor's main papyrus. It should be noted that another separate document of the same kind was written for the sister of Paiuhor.[205]

204 Allen 1974, 82 (T 1).

205 Louvre N 3192a; see Mekis 2019, 260 with n. 16.

Chapter 13

Amuletic necklace

13.1. The necklace

Around the neck of Djedhor was fastened a string of amulets in blue faience, gilt wood, and ivory (or bone). This is mentioned in the autopsy report by Pleyte under nos. M 47b.16a–y. In the inventory book the various amulets were registered as AL 1–35, with the knot in the string as no. AL 36. The latter cannot be found nowadays, and neither can some of the amulets, such as the bulb of garlic, two of the stairs, the three stone heart amulets, and one of the ivory *wedjat eyes*. It should be noted that in the *procès-verbal* there is some confusion about the used materials: the *tyet* and *menat* amulets, stairs, and Sons of Horus (four baboon-headed figures!) are actually of blue faience; the small *wedjat* and the *aper* are of bone or ivory; the rest has been made of gilt wood. Clearly, the use of this latter material can be regarded as yet another instance of the substitution of rather fragile substances in funerary jewellery, instead of the more sturdy alternatives employed for everyday life.[206] The headrest is described by Pleyte as being of haematite, though the inventory book mentions 'fired earth' (i.e. faience or terracotta). The amuletic necklace has been restrung in random order in 1993, with three heart amulets of unknown provenance to replace the unidentifiable original ones (Fig. 31).

A similar amuletic necklace was found by Migliarini on the mummy of Takerheb now in Florence.[207] His autopsy report terminates with a full list of the amulets found on the body,[208] including a figure of Isis, a falcon, a heart amulet, a *djed* pillar, a *wedjat* eye, and a headrest, similar to the Leiden set of Djedhor. In addition, Takerheb's necklace had figurines of Thoth, Re, and Imhotep, a uraeus, feather, and lotus flower, all of them lacking in Djedhor's necklace.[209] It should be noted that several of these amulets were again made of gilt wood, which seems to be a characteristic material for the period in question. More amulets were found elsewhere on Takerheb's body: a lotus or papyrus above the left eye, two feathers above the brow,[210] a *djed* pillar on the right side, and a seal or square under the armpit (the latter may have slipped off a finger, since the arms lay crossed over the chest; see below, § 13.2). X-ray photographs of the two mummies of Hornedjitef and Horemheb in the British Museum likewise indicate the presence of numerous amulets on the upper chest.[211] The mummy of Neswaiu in Stockholm possessed no less that 120 amulets on the chest area, including a larger specimen in gold depicting a falcon with outspread wings

206 Cf. a similar case *supra* in § 11.1 (anklets). For gilt wood, cf. Petrie 1914, 10 (heart, breast), 15 (*menat*). Cf. also gilt wax or gold foil used for other funerary amulets instead of solid gold.
207 Birch 1855, 165.
208 Birch 1855, 169. Cf. Guidotti 2003.
209 A slightly different list is given by Guidotti 2009, 24–25, including *tyet*, *menat* and *aper*.
210 Cf. Elias/Mekis 2019, 148 and fig. 4b-1 no. 2.
211 Dawson/Gray 1968, 24 no. 44, 26 no. 48.

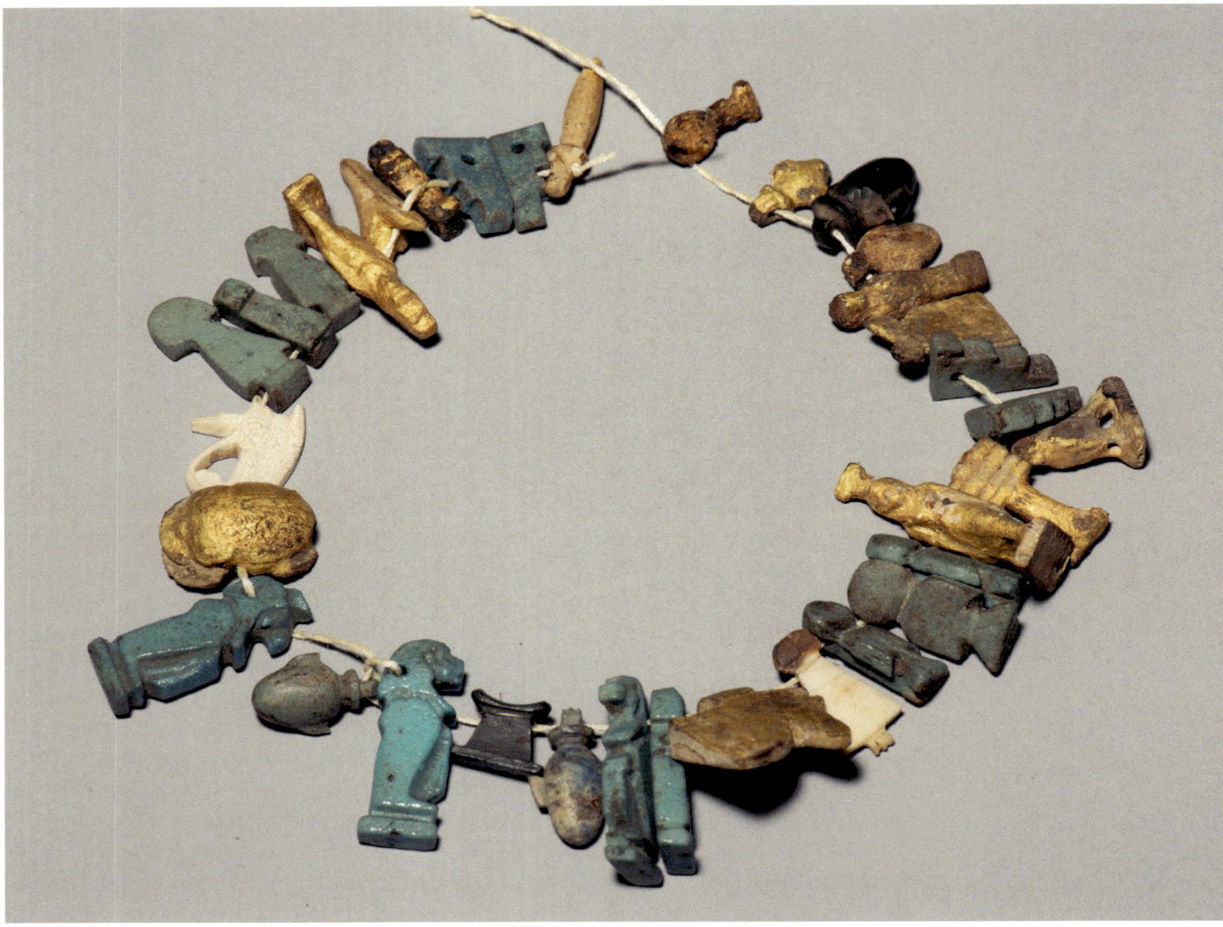

Fig. 31. Amuletic necklace as restrung (RMO, inv. AL 1–35).

(which was reproduced in a digital manner).[212] A similar array of amulets was found on the mummy of Tarepyt in Cairo during recent CT-scans.[213]

13.2. Other amulets

Otherwise, Djedhor's autopsy report mentions yet another bulb of garlic or perhaps small onion in one of the fists (no. M47b.19) and a small plaque of ivory stuck onto the left-hand ring-finger by way of a ring bezel (no. M 47b.18). The bezel cannot be retrieved in the present museum collections, but the bulb of garlic or onion still exists (inv. no. AL 63 = L.XII.2-c). The recent scan of the mummy of Hornedjitef in London showed the presence of a finger ring, possibly with bezel, on the left hand, and of a plain metal ring around the left big toe.[214] We have already referred above to the possibility that also Takerheb in Florence originally may have had a seal on one of her fingers. The placing of a gold ring on a finger of the left hand is explicitly prescribed by the Ritual of Embalming.[215] The use of onions inside the mummy wrappings is not uncommon,[216] whereas several sources report on the custom to wear a garland of onions around the neck during the Sokar feast.[217] Possibly, the garlic (or onion?) found by Pleyte among the amulets of the necklace is connected with this ritual.

212 See https://www.bbc.com/news/technology-26664927.

213 Elias/Mekis 2019, 147–151 with fig. 4c-1.

214 Filer 1999, 100.

215 Töpfer 2017, 26, Chapter x + X. Cf. also Elias/Mekis 2019, 151.

216 Germer 1985, 192; cf. Töpfer 2017, 30 n. 55 (quoting Granville).

217 Keimer 1984, 56 with n. 36.

Chapter 14

Inner wrappings

14.1. Fragmentary shrouds

Due to the presence of various layers of hard bituminous or resinous material, Pleyte found it impossible to remove all the linen wrappings in a systematic manner. Instead, numerous linen bandages and shrouds could only be cut up into pieces or extracted as loose fragments. Thus, it is often not clear whether such fragments originally formed larger entities (or shrouds), and how such textiles were distributed over the mummy. A similar situation prevailed during the Florence autopsy, so that the two reports can only present a tantalizing impression of the wrappings. Nowadays, the Leiden collections preserve numerous isolated samples which can only partly be identified with concrete items mentioned in Pleyte's *procès-verbal*.

Under no. 47b.12, Pleyte mentions the remains of a large shroud decorated with several small vignettes. The first five samples were given inv.nos. AL 44a–e and have been published in a recent catalogue of the Leiden textile collection (Fig. 32a–e).[218] They have been drawn in black ink with the addition of some yellow and red pigment. According to the editors of the catalogue, the thread count of these five fragments is almost the same (except for no. 155, but this may be a mistake), so indeed they may have been parts of one and the same shroud. The vignettes in question depict a vulture with a phallus, a uraeus on top of a stair, a serpent in a shrine, a short kilt, and what may be a crocodile's tail. Next Pleyte mentions three more fragments (f–h), depicting part of a woman or goddess, the lower part of a man, and again part of a woman, respectively; these samples cannot be identified in the present-day collections.[219] Instead of forming parts of one large shroud, all these samples may have been separate linen amulets instead.

Number 47b.13 of the autopsy report concerns part of the image of a goddess, identified by Pleyte as Nephthys. This was registered as no. AL 39 in the inventory books. It depicts no more than the abdomen and foreward arm of a standing female in black ink, and therefore the identification as Nephthys cannot be confirmed nowadays. The fragment was mounted on cardboard together with autopsy no. M 47b.14, identified as the legs and kilt of a standing king, which indeed is corroborated by the presence of a sporran with uraei (Fig. 33). It was registered as no. AL 41 in the inventory books. Four minor fragments were stuck onto the same cardboard panel, which has no. 151 in the textile catalogue.[220] One of

218 Van 't Hooft *et al.* 1994, 81–82 nos. 153–157 with pl. 7. The inventory book no. 13, page 14 mentions five numbers AL 44a–d (i.e. AL 44, plus four more nos. a–d), which is confusing and has been corrected to 44a–e in the modern digital registration.

219 Although the frame M 47b.13.14 (mentioned below as the next item; Fig. 33) has pencil numbers f and g added to two of the samples, probably incorrectly because the missing fragments of M 47b.12 should be polychromous, and the samples on frame M 47b.13.14 are just black line-drawings. Perhaps the missing samples can be identified with three unknown fragments with indistinct line drawings stuck onto cardboard M 47b.30.34 (see Fig. 43, cat.no. 178).

220 Van 't Hooft *et al.* 1994, 80–81 no. 151 with pl. 7.

Fig. 32a–e. Five vignettes on linen (RMO, inv. AL 44a–e).

Fig. 33. Six linen fragments with parts of vignettes (RMO, inv. AL 39 and 41).

Fig. 34. Six linen fragments with parts of vignettes (RMO, inv. AL 45).

these seems to depict a profile view of the head of Osiris with *atef* crown and concentric collar, the other three are unclear. All six fragments appear to have more or less the same thread count, a bit coarser than the above-mentioned fragments of autopsy no. 12.

Pleyte's autopsy report next mentions, under no. 15, a 'painted shroud ... with polychrome depictions of the figures of several gods and goddesses, but now unrecognizable due to the infiltration of the bitumen'. Indeed, the inventory book, under nos. AL 45a–e, also mentions six fragments of such a shroud with divine figures. These fragments were mounted on another cardboard frame, labelled M 47b.15 and catalogued as no. 158 (Fig. 34).[221] They comprise partial depictions of a standing goddess facing left with a headdress of cow's horns, the legs of two men facing in opposite directions, adoring hands directed to the right, a standing mummy facing left and another standing figure facing in the opposite direction.[222] All vignettes are executed in black with details in yellow.

14.2. Artificial breasts

The next textile item on the autopsy list is no. 20, described as linen braces slung around the neck and inscribed with the name and titles of the deceased. These cannot be identified among the present-day collections, although they may be hiding among the numerous other inscribed bandages discussed above in Chapter 10 (inv. AL 51, especially vel 5). Pleyte's no. 21 is described as a shroud with gilt nipples, with under it (no. 24) an articial fill of the breasts made up of various fragments of linen and including 'artificial nipples made of textile'. These two items were mounted

221 Van 't Hooft *et al.* 1994, 82 no. 158 (no illustration).

222 For parallels from contemporary mummies, cf. Schreiber 2007, 351 figs. 25–28.

Fig. 35. Linen fragments of two artificial breasts and a shroud with gilt nipples (RMO, inv. L.XII.2-l).

on a common panel of cardboard labelled M 47b.21.24, catalogued as no. 147 but not mentioned as such in the inventory book (Fig. 35).[223] It has now been registered as inv.no. L.XII.2-l. More remains of the filling material are now kept under a separate number, inv.no. L.XII 2-m.[224]

223 Van 't Hooft *et al.* 1994, 79–80 no. 147.
224 Van 't Hooft *et al.* 1994, 80 no. 148.

Though it is remarkable that a male mummy such as Djedher's should have such pronounced breasts and nipples, parallels of this custom to enhance the breasts in a male individual have been observed for several mummies dating to the Roman Period. Thus two mummies in Leiden have the nipples accentuated by dots of resin (inv.nos.

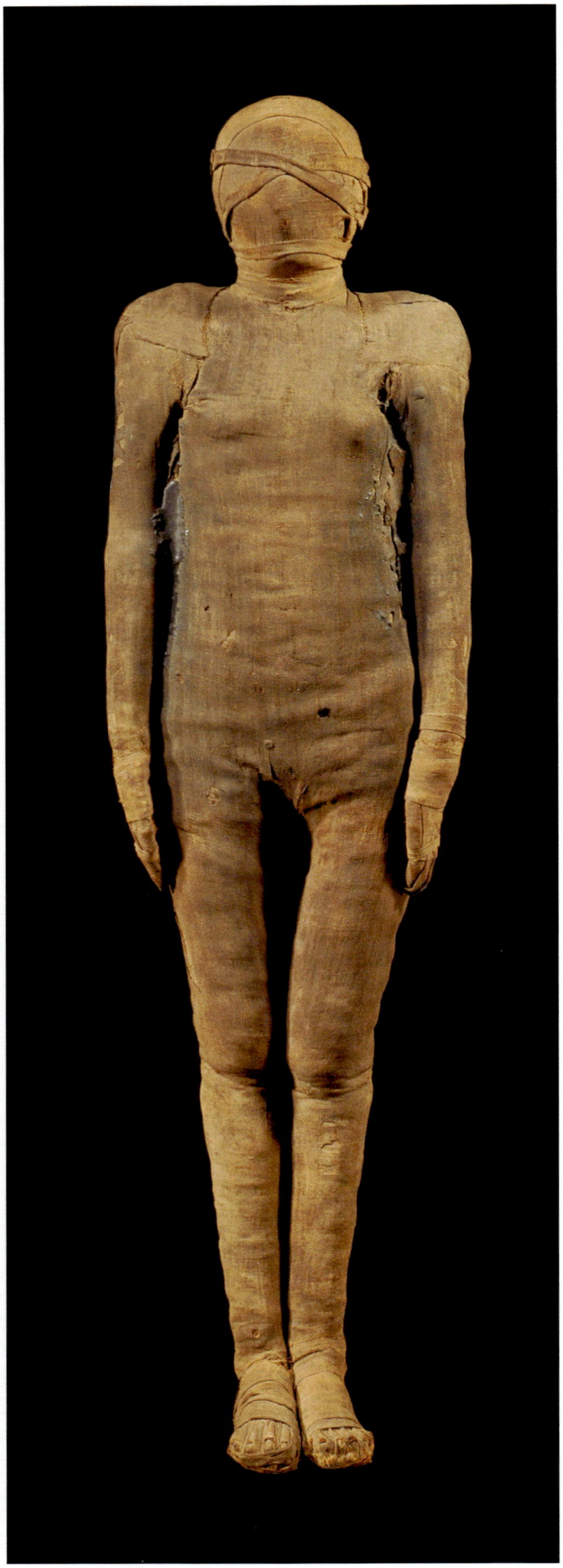

Fig. 36. Male mummy with female characteristics (RMO, inv. AMM 10).

AMM 25-b and AMM 24-a, or mummy cat. 29–30).[225] The nipples could also be indicated by small disks in gilt wax, such as they are present in the Leiden collection.[226] Perhaps two of these belonged to the Roman Period mummy cat. 29, [227] and in that case the resinous dots on the exterior shroud were merely the attachment for gilt disks. A third Leiden mummy (inv.no. AMM 10-e, cat. 31) has linen padding on the chest and around the hips to suggest a female contour (Fig. 36), although it has been sexed as male on the basis of radiological evidence.[228] A male mummy with padded breasts dating to the same period is also present in the British Museum (EA 6704).[229] A special case is the so-called mummy of Butehamon, formerly in Brussels until the autopsy by Jonckheere.[230] Although this mummy was attributed to Dynasty XXI in view of its sarcophagus inscribed for Butehamon, it has in fact several characteristics of Roman date, including artificial breasts.[231]

Thus far, no convincing explanation has been given for this puzzling sexual dimorphism. Parallels which spring to mind are of course the androgynous depictions of the Nile god Hapy, which are usually explained as a symbolic reference to this god's status as both father and mother of creation.[232] Likewise, the androgynous representation of Akhenaten in some of his Karnak colossi is often interpreted as a sign of the King's association with yet another demiurge, viz. the god Atum.[233] Again in this case, the dual masculine and feminine qualities embodied in the creator god seem to have reflected the fertility of nature. It is unclear to which extent this kind of symbolism can

---

225 Raven/Taconis 2005, 193 with fig. 3b, 198 with figs. 3a and 3d.

226 Raven 1984, 22 with n. 247, 38 nos. 40–44 and pl. 7.

227 Raven/Taconis 2005, 191 (three gold leaf amulets mentioned in the Anastasi catalogue, so that the third one may have represented the navel).

228 *Ibid.*, 201–202 with figs. 3a and 3e.

229 Dawson/Gray 1968, 33–34 with pl. 17b; Taylor 2001, 91 with fig. 53.

230 Jonckheere 1942.

231 *Ibid.*, 67. Other characteristics are a shroud leaving the head, feet and hands uncovered and set off with a painted band below, the separately wrapped arms, legs, fingers and toes, and the decorative patterns of the wrappings on the face. On the other hand, the arms crossed over the chest seem to point to a Ptolemaic date. The absence of typical details peculiar for the Third Intermediate Period was already noted by Jonckheere himself (*Op.cit.*, 128). On the whole, the mummy seems to be an early example of the group of Roman mummies mentioned by Raven/Taconis 2005, 195, 199, 203. The addition of an earlier coffin (either during the original interment or added by the 19th-century dealers) is also typical for this group.

232 Cf. D. Kurth, in: LÄ IV.485, *s.v. Nilgott*; W. Westendorf, in: LÄ II.633–635, *s.v. Götter, androgyne*.

233 Cf. R.E. Freed, in: Freed/Markowitz/D'Auria 1999, 113–114 with ns. 12–15.

be relevant for the interpretation of the above-mentioned mummies of private persons dating to the Graeco-Roman Period. However, various details of their apparel, especially the decorations at the head end of the cartonnage covers and masks, hint at a close association with the sun god.[234] Another religious concept highly important at the time is that of the *Gliedervergottung*: the assimilation of the various limbs with specific gods, concluding with the statement that 'there is no member in him which lacks a god'.[235] Thus here, too, the ambivalent gender expression may be a sign of the deceased's prevailing identity with the creator god (or: with all gods). It should be noted that Djedhor's mummy is earlier than the others showing this ambivalent gender, which appear to be Roman in date, and so far is the oldest specimen showing this remarkable dimorphism.

14.3. Assorted textiles

Autopsy number 22 refers to more parallel bandages, with no. 23 being reserved for a bandage inscribed in black ink with a demotic text. It has been mounted together with the hieratic bandages of panel AL 51 vel 5 (see Fig. 23), erroneously labelled as M 47b.20 (Fig. 37). This bandage was registered in the inventory book as no. AL 59. The interpretation of this text presents several problems. A note in Pleyte's handwriting in the RMO archives[236] suggests a reading 'the seat of the heart of Kehaubu', implying a reference to Djedhor's mother Takerheb which would be very surprising. An alternative reading *tꜣ st ꜣꜣ.ty n tꜣ ḫryt-ib* 'The seat/place of the heart is in the interior of the body' was suggested by Holger Kockelmann[237] and has been confirmed by Petra Hogenboom. The 'interior of the body' might refer to the thoracic cavity, and the text might be meant as an instruction for the gods who had to weigh the heart of the deceased in the hereafter, revealing to them where to find it. Possibly, the text is at least partly identical to an inscription on a bandage found on the Florence mummy by Migliarini.[238]

Pleyte's number 25 concerns more 'filling and cross-bands'. These fragments were stuck onto a cardboard panel as the others, labelled M47b.25 and registered as inv.no. AL 50a-d (Fig. 38).[239] They consist of a group of five overlapping bands, two single pieces, and two groups of bandages applied cross-wise.

More interesting is autopsy no. 26, representing the goddess Isis facing right, with her name sign on the head, the left hand raised and holding a basket surmounted by a *wedjat* eye, and the right hand held in a gesture of veneration. This was registered in the inventory books as inv.no. AL 40 and in the later textile catalogue as no. 150.[240] The figure has been drawn in black outlines only and displays the characteristic Ptolemaic rendering of the female body (Fig. 39).

Less clear is the situation with Pleyte's numbers 27 (a girdle of braces and cross-bands, perhaps meant to be an imitation of the traditional 'stola' of the god Osiris) and 28 (three shrouds). The inventory book simply mentions unspecified 'samples of linen' and 'samples of bandages' under nos. AL 48–49, which is of no help in identifying these remains among the present-day collections. However, there are two parts of a single (?) large shroud with end bands and long fringes in bleached linen (inv.nos. L.XII.2-f and -k, Fig. 40),[241] and a large fragment of a red linen shroud (inv. no. L.XII.2-e, Fig. 41)[242] which bear labels connecting them with Djedhor's mummy. Perhaps they can be regarded as Pleyte's number M47b.28, with the two bleached linen fragments counting as two separate shrouds.

The 'wrappings of fine byssus' mentioned by Pleyte under autopsy number 30 can be identified as inventory number L.XII.2-a and have been catalogued as textile no. 145.[243] These consist of two fragments of very fine, undyed cloth with a thread count of 50 × 16 per cm^2 (Fig. 42). The use of very fine linen for the layers close to the skin is quite common in mummification.

The remaining textiles were only sampled by Pleyte, who stuck parts of various bandages on a piece of cardboard labelled M47b.30.34 (Fig. 43). This label is doubtless incorrect, and in fact the samples in question seem to represent autopsy nos. 31–34bis. These have now been registered as nos. 160–178 in the textile catalogue (original inventory no. AL 48). They include samples of linen of various qualities (autopsy number 31 = cat. 171–176), samples of sewing (autopsy number 32 = cat. 160, 162), samples of mending (autopsy number 33 = cat. 168–170, 177), three bandages stuck together with resin (autopsy number 34 = cat. 166), and samples of bandages with ink marks (autopsy number 34bis = cat. 161, 163–165, 167).[244] The ink marks in question cannot be read as either hieratic or demotic, and may be of a different character instead.[245] A provisional suggestion would be that these are location marks referring to the correct deposition of these wrappings on the body of the deceased.

234 Cf. Hellinckx 2002, Chapter 4.
235 *Ibid.*, 213.
236 Archives RMO, 6.4.3/3 *sub* 2.1.1 (box C93). This reading is rejected by Sven Vleeming, in a letter of 3-4-1992 preserved in the same archive box.
237 Kockelmann 2008, 229–230 with n. 40.
238 Birch 1855, pl. XV.D, reproduced in Raven 1993, fig. 95.
239 Van 't Hooft *et al.* 1994, 88 no. 181.
240 Van 't Hooft *et al.* 1994, 80 no. 150 with pl. 6.
241 Van 't Hooft *et al.* 1994, 78–79 nos. 143–144.
242 Van 't Hooft *et al.* 1994, 78 no. 142.
243 Van 't Hooft *et al.* 1994, 78 no. 145.
244 For the three remaining samples (cat. no. 178), see above, n. 219.
245 I thank Petra Hogenboom for her help.

Fig. 37. Linen bandage with demotic inscription (RMO, inv. AL 59).

Fig. 38. Samples of bandages (RMO, inv. AL 50).

Fig. 39. Partial shroud with figure of Isis (RMO, inv. AL 40).

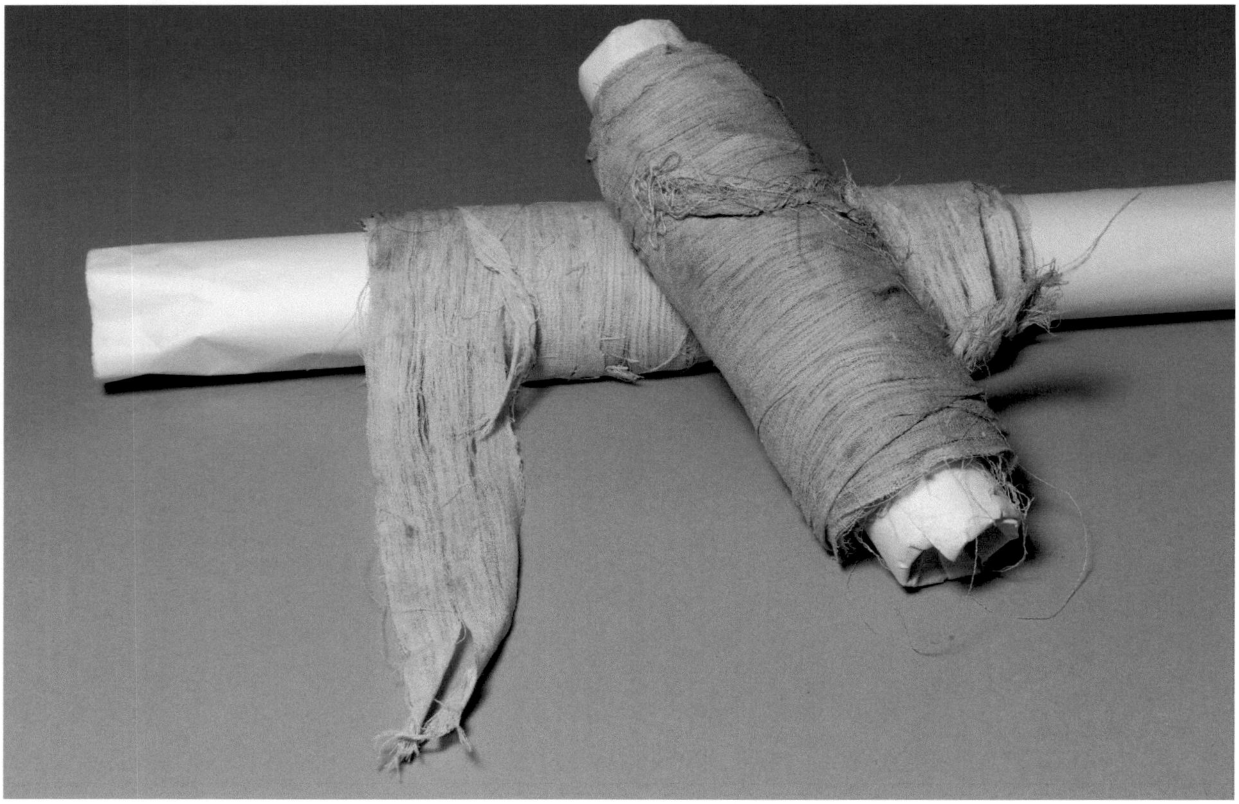

Fig. 40 (opposite page). Two fragments of a bleached linen shroud (RMO, inv. L.XII.2-f and –k).

Fig. 42 (opposite page). Fragments of fine linen (RMO, inv. L.XII.2-a).

Fig. 41. Fragment of a red linen shroud (RMO, inv. L.XII.2-e).

Fig. 43. Various samples of linen (RMO, inv. AL 48): lower row from left to right cat. 166, 162, 160, 161 (left) and 167 (right), 163–164 and 165 (2x); second row cat.nos. 177, 168–170; third row cat. no. 178 (3x); upper row cat.nos. 171–175 and 176 (2x).

Fig. 44. Rolled-up bandage fragments (RMO, inv. L.XII.2-j).

Fig. 45. Rolled-up bandage (RMO, inv. AL 49-a).

Fig. 46. Four bandages (RMO, inv. L.XII.2-n).

Next, Pleyte mentions 'several samples of bandages, all taken from the thighs where they had been best preserved. One is complete, there are narrower and wider ones' (autopsy no. 35). Perhaps these are identical to the bandages registered in the inventory book as AL 49. They may be identified as a number of neatly rolled-up bandages now kept in the museum's reserves: catalogue numbers 141 (with extra inventory number L.XII.2-j, Fig. 44), 179 (inv. AL 49-b), and 180 (inv. AL 49-a, Fig. 45). Four other bandage fragments (cat.no. 146, inv. L.XII.2-n, labelled M47b.35) are now kept in a separate plastic bag (Fig. 46), whereas a second bag contains the much decayed remains of numerous bandages (inv.no. L.XII.2-o, not catalogued).

Fig. 47. Navel (RMO, inv. L.XII.2-i).

14.4. Navel

The last item found during the unwrapping of the mummy of Djedhor is described by Pleyte as a circular filling (autopsy no. 36). This has the present inventory number L.XII.2-i and has been catalogued as no. 140 (Fig. 47). It is a disc of 3.5 cm in diameter, made of several layers of linen, flat above and slightly concave below, and carrying the label M47b.36. Doubtless, it can be identified as a depiction of the deceased's navel. In Graeco-Roman mummies, the accentuation of the navel is a regularly occurring phenomenon. Like the nipples,[246] the navel can be indicated by a gilded wax disk. Several such disks may be found in the RMO collections.[247] Alternatives are star-shaped or disk-shaped amulets of faience.[248] Roman mummies occasionally have a ring- or doughnut-shaped object made of linen, deposited on the abdomen directly under the exterior shroud.[249] The navel was of course reminiscent of the moment of birth, and hence also of rebirth. Texts indicate the association of the navel with the morning star (Venus),[250] which suggests that the deceased would be reborn as a star (or as Re) at the beginning of creation.[251]

Finally, Pleyte mentions how he extracted some resin from the mummy's skull by heating (autopsy report no. 38). This sample received inventory number AL 64 and is still kept in the museum's reserves as a patch of resin of 9.8 × 9.8 cm stuck onto paper and labelled M47b.38 (Fig. 48). As remarked above in Chapter 6, M 47c.1 would perhaps be a more appropriate number for this item.

Fig. 48. Resin (RMO, inv. AL 64).

246 See *supra*, § 14.2.
247 Raven 1984, 22 with n. 247, 38 nos. 40–44 and pl. 7.
248 Hellinckx 2002, 289.
249 Raven/Taconis 2005, 188–190 with fig. 4c (inv. AMM 9), 193–195 with figs.3c, 4a–b (inv. AMM 25-b), 198–199 with figs. 3b and 3d (inv. AMM 24-a). Hellinckx 2002, 289, n. 2317 refers to a similar find on a Ptolemaic mummy in Cracow (inv. AS/2438; see Niwiński 1998), I.184, pl. 1.2).
250 Hellinckx 2002, 289–295.
251 *Ibid.*, 294–295.

14.5. Parallels

It is interesting to compare these textiles from the Djedhor mummy with those of Takerheb in Florence. During the autopsy in Florence, Migliarini likewise found several pieces of linen bearing designs in ink, though these were rather different from the ones found by Pleyte. Above, in Chapter 10, we have already referred to Takerheb's exterior shroud, the two outer layers of bituminous substances, and the inscribed bandages and Osiris shroud found in between. Fragments of such an Osiris shroud were also found by Pleyte (inv. AL 38, Fig. 25). Such shrouds with large figures of Osiris became a regular feature of Egyptian mummies in the Roman Period,[252] but Ptolemaic Period specimens are also known.[253] They occasionally include large figures of Isis or Nephthys supporting the central figure of Osiris,[254] or smaller depictions ranged in several registers to either side. It cannot be excluded that part of the other linen vignettes removed by Pleyte during his autopsy (and now kept in the reserve collections under inventory numbers AL 40, 44-45; here Figs. 32, 34, 39) belonged in fact to the same Osiris shroud. However, according to the textile catalogue the thread count is different for all these fragments, which would preclude their belonging to one single piece of textile.[255]

Under the second bituminous layer, Migliarini found a shroud with a panther skin design and a representation of the *imy-wet* symbol.[256] Parallels with a panther skin motif have been found in TT 32 in the Theban necropolis.[257] The head of the Florence mummy had been wrapped in narrow bands forming recessed cells of a rhombic pattern, a favourite technique of Graeco-Roman mummies.[258] Some of the bandages had been inscribed with texts. Underneath, the head had been covered with several square pieces of linen, fastened with a fillet of twisted threads. There was an amulet in the shape of two feathers on the forehead, as well as three square pieces of linen with the design of the crowns of Upper and Lower Egypt.[259] Two similar squares lay on the eyes, inscribed with a design of the two sacred eyes of the pantheistic Amun of Chapter 163 from the Book of the Dead, as already remarked by Birch.[260] Yet another square lay on the occiput of the head, with a design of adoring baboons in a border of rams' heads.[261] All this shows what may have been lost in the extensive resinous layer covering Djedhor's head.

More pieces of cloth with designs were found on Takerheb's body.[262] These included two Osiris figures in shrines (right and left); a figure of Thoth presenting a *wedjat* eye, and a large Nephthys on the same strip of linen (right); a figure of Maʿat; a Sokaris falcon; part of an Anubis jackal; and two crocodiles (right and left, near the feet). Only the Nephthys and the crocodiles can be compared to the Djedhor mummy (Figs. 32–33). Finally, two text columns in hieroglyphs had been inscribed vertically along the thighs, apparently giving the identity of the deceased.[263]

252 Bresciani 1996, 15 (type 1).
253 Parlasca 1966, 157–159; Schreiber 2007, 340–341, 352–353.
254 Parlasca 1966, pl. 57.2; Bresciani 1996, figs. 64–65.
255 Cf. Van 't Hooft *et al.* 1994, cat. nos. 149–150, 153–158.
256 For the following, see Birch 1855, 163–165. Now retrieved in Christchurch, New Zealand: Rosati 2013, 219.
257 Schreiber 2007, 341–342, 354.
258 For two other mummy heads of the same period with a very careful wrapping pattern, see Jonckheere 1942, 62 with fig. 29; Marshall/Lichtenberg 2013, fig. 55 (Louvre N 2627).
259 Now retrieved in Christchurch, New Zealand: Rosati 2013, 219. Cf. Schreiber 2007, 339, 349.
260 Birch 1855, 170–171 n. 6. Cf. Rosati 2003, 45 n. 3; reproduced by Guidotti 2009, fig. 1.
261 Birch 1855, 165; reproduced by Guidotti 2009, fig. 2; now in Christchurch: Rosati 2009, 9. For such hypocephali of abnormal type, see Schreiber 2007, 342 and figs. 49–53.
262 Birch 1855, 166.
263 Birch 1855, 166, pl. XV no. E; reproduced in Raven 1993, fig. 95.

Chapter 15

Mummification techniques

Above, mention has already been made of the extensive application of resinous materials applied on the exterior of the wrappings, as well as on a number of lower strata of the bandages. This seems to be a characteristic of Ptolemaic mummies in general, which often have a shiny black appearance and a considerable weight. Pleyte was unable to open the mummy and examine its interior condition, due to the destructive effects of the resinous fluids poured over the body during the embalming process. A similar situation prevailed in Florence, where Migliarini refrained from removing the lower layers of the bandages and the flesh.[264] This has deprived us of information on the mummification techniques employed on these bodies.

Some more details are available for the two mummies in London, which were X-rayed instead.[265] Hornedjitef was wrapped in 'vast amounts of linen'.[266] Both Horemheb and Hornedjitef proved to have four cylindrical packages of linen and resin inside the thoracic and abdominal cavities, doubtless based on the four intestinal packages of former times,[267] although the recent scans of Hornedjitef's mummy seem to suggest that the packages may rather contain statuettes.[268] Similar packages have been detected on the scans of the mummy of Neswaiu now in Stockholm.[269] Presumably, the 'rolled pieces' mentioned by Pleyte in the *procès-verbal* (*sub* 37) also concerned such cylindrical packages.

The presence of intestinal packages inside the mummy is rather remarkable, since the funerary custom to deposit the separately embalmed intestines inside the abdominal cavity had gone out of fashion several centuries before these mummies were made, as argued by Dawson and Gray.[270] More usual was the alternative tradition of depositing the four packages inside a naos-shaped canopic box of painted wood.[271] We shall see in § 16.4 that several of the comparative burials used here as parallels to Djedhor's in fact possessed such boxes: yet another traditional feature of these burials that one may regard as redundant,[272] and indeed some of these boxes have been shown to contain no more than a few potsherds wrapped in linen. The presence of cylindrical packages of intestines has been detected inside other contemporary or even later mummies.[273] This practice is explicitly prescribed

264 Birch 1855, 167.
265 Cf. also the recent scans of the mummy of Tarepyt in Cairo: Elias/Mekis 2019, 146 ff.
266 Filer 1999, 99–100.
267 Dawson/Gray 1968, 24 no. 44, 26 no. 48.
268 Filer 1999, 99.
269 See https://www.bbc.com/news/technology-26664927.
270 Dawson/Gray 1968, 24 no. 44.
271 Cf. Ikram/Dodson 1998, 292 with fig. 438; Aston 2010, especially 167–175, type C2.
272 Cf. the remark about the Book of the Dead texts in § 12.2 above.
273 Raven/Taconis 2005, Cat. 20–21, 29, 31. Cf. Elias/Mekis 2019, 146–147.

in the Ritual of Embalming.[274] The mummy of Horemheb in London shows a clear incision in the left side for the removal of the internal organs.[275]

The Florence mummy has a perforation in the orbit of the right eye. According to Birch, this must have been made for the extraction of the brain.[276] Although this is a rather unusual place for such a perforation, he points out that there are other exceptions to the rule that excerebration took place via the nose.[277] It is also possible that the damaged orbital wall merely was the result of excerebration executed in a negligent way.[278] Proof of excerebration was also found in Hornedjitef's mummy in London, which proved to have a clear fluid level of resin in the occiput of the otherwise empty skull.[279]

Another feature which all these five mummies have in common is the position of the arms, which lie crossed over the chest in all cases.[280] This is in fact another characteristic of Ptolemaic mummies in general, not just restricted to the Theban area.[281] Of course, this posture is reminescent of that of the god Osiris himself, who is generally depicted as holding the crook and flail of his kingship of the hereafter. It is a clear sign of the association of Djedhor's body with that of Osiris – already expressed by the depiction on one of his shrouds (Fig. 25) – and thereby yet another manifestation of the conviction that the deceased would be resurrected. The gilding of the nails of hands and feet, as seen on the mummy of Djedhor, and sometimes also of other areas of the skin, is also typical of the period in question.[282] This, too, is a sign of the divine status of the deceased, since according to the Egyptians the flesh of the gods consisted of gold and gilding was therefore an effective means to express divinity and immortality.[283]

Above, we have already commented on two other peculiarities of Djedhor's mummy: the androgynous appearance of the chest area (§ 14.2) and the accentuation of the navel (§ 14.4). Both phenomena have been recognized as indications that the mummy of the deceased was assimilated with the demiurge, who – as a unique god – was father and mother of creation at the same time. This ensured Djedhor's daily rebirth with Re at dawn and the eternal preservation of his body.

274 Töpfer 2017, 25, Chapter x + VI.

275 Cf. Elias/Mekis 2019, 146 *sub* 5.

276 Birch 1855, 167.

277 One case is illustrated in Jonckheere 1942, 87 fig. 41.

278 Raven/Taconis 2005, 36, 163, 174, 182, 211.

279 Filer 1999, 99. Cf. Elias/Mekis 2019, 146 *sub* 3 and fig. 4b-1.

280 Birch 1855, 166; Dawson/Gray 1968, 24 no. 44, 26 no. 48; https://www.bbc.com/news/technology-26664927.

281 Gray 1972, 200–201; Raven/Taconis 2005, 157; cf. Töpfer 2017, 28–30; Elias/Mekis 2019, 149 and fig. 4c-1.

282 Raven/Taconis 2005, 157 and Cat. 23, 41, and 44; for gilded nails, see especially Hellinckx 2002, 20–22; Töpfer 2017, 25 Chapter x + VII, 31. See already above, § 11.3.

283 Cf. D. Arnold, in: LÄ II.7565 *s.v. Goldverkleidung*; L. Störk, in: LÄ II.729 *s.v. Gold.*

Chapter 16

Other burial gifts

16.1. The standard funerary ensemble

Apart from the mummy and cartonnage, Djedhor's burial must have contained a number of other funerary items. Above, we have already seen that the original coffin was replaced by a specimen belonging to a different individual, presumably by the art robbers of the 19th century.[284] Quite probably, an individual with an elevated social status like Djedhor possessed even two coffins originally, an outer and an inner one (§ 16.2). Contemporary elite burials comprised a number of additional funerary items as well. Thus the head of the mummy was often lying on a hypocephalus (§ 16.3), and the mummy's intestines had been deposited in a wooden canopic box (§ 16.4).[285] Next to the coffin stood a wooden Ptah-Sokar-Osiris statue holding a miniature corn-mummy as a magic aid for the resurrection (§ 16.5). Elsewhere in the burial chamber must have stood a funerary stela, likewise made of painted wood (§ 16.6): the use of costly stone was not necessary, since these stelae were no longer exposed to the elements in the tomb's superstructure.

Some of these items of Djedhor's burial may have survived in collections outside Leiden,[286] where at least two of them can be retrieved on the basis of the extant inscriptions, but other items seem to have been lost. Comparison with other contemporary burials may help to reconstruct those items. Below, we shall focus on those comparative burials for which there are cartonnages of similar type (see above, § 7.2), as this appears to be the most reliable method (see Table 3).

16.2. Coffins

In § 4.2 above, mention has been made of the non-matching coffin of a man Irhapiaut in which Djedhor's mummy arrived in the Leiden museum (see also Fig. 10). Presumably, this indicates that Djedhor's original coffins were already lost due to decay when his tomb was found, and that the dealers involved in this find provided another coffin in order to make a better price for Djedhor's mummy on the contemporary art market. Comparative evidence indicates that Djedhor must once have possessed not one, but even two wooden coffins. Such coffins are still preserved for the following individuals:

284 § 4.2 with fig. 10.

285 If the intestines had been returned to the abdominal cavity instead, the box was occasionally added to the burial for purely traditional reasons. In this case, it sometimes contained packages of potsherds wrapped in linen. See above, Chapter 15.

286 For a candidate for Djedhor's bead net, see above, Chapter 9 with n. 155 and Fig. 19.

owner	outer coffin	inner coffin	cartonnage	bead net	hypocephalus	canopic box	PSO figure	stela
Djedhor			Lei L.XII.2-d	Lou N 3078 ?		Lou N 2644	Lou AF 708	
Hornedjitef	BM EA 6677	BM EA 6678	BM EA 6679		BM EA 8446	Lei AH 215	BM EA 9736	
Nehemsyrattaway			Avign. A 67A		Phil. 29.86.436		Lou N 3510 E	
Neswaiu	MM E.6	MM E.7	MM E.5				BM EA 9737	BM EA 8468
Nestanetjeretten			Lou AF 12859		ME C. 2324		Lou N 3508 E + 3520 B	ME C. 1599
Paiuhor			Paisley EG 203, 212, 239		ME C. 2321	Herm. 822	Lou N 3520 A + 2514 B	ME C. 1569
Takerheb		MA 5703 A	MA 5703 B		MA 5704			

Table 3. Composition of burial ensembles of most prominent Ptolemaic burials. Abbreviations: Avign. = Musée Calvet, Avignon; BM = British Museum, London; Herm. = Hermitage Museum, St. Petersburg; Lei = National Museum of Antiquities, Leiden; Lou = Musée du Louvre, Paris; MA = Museo Archeologico, Florence; ME = Museo Egizio, Turin; MM = Medelhavsmuseet (now Världskulturmuseerna), Stockholm; Paisley = Paisley Museum, Paisley; Penn. = Pennsylvania Museum, Philadelphia.

- Hornedjitef, London, British Museum, EA 6677–6678, outer and inner coffin (Figs. 49–50).[287]
- Neswaiu, Stockholm, Världskulturmuseerna, E.6–7, outer and inner coffin.[288]
- Takerheb, Florence, Museo Archeologico, 5703 A, inner coffin only.[289]

The exterior coffins in question are black with yellow painted details and have a plinth under the feet and a remarkable square outline of the head.[290] Such plinths or pedestals, in conjunction with the back-pillars, rather gave these coffins the appearance of an Osiride statue, like the contemporary Ptah-Sokar-Osiris statues.[291] Regardless of the question whether the coffins were actually positioned on their feet – for instance during the last rites of the Opening of the Mouth during the burial ceremonies – these features probably symbolized the imminent resurrection of the deceased. The prevailing black colour of the decoration is likewise a symbol of the netherworld as a place of resurrection.[292] The details in yellow or gold may be regarded as a reference to the nocturnal passing of the solar disk through the netherworld, which revivified its inhabitants and briefly allowed them to see their surroundings.

The inner coffins are much more elegant but likewise have a square head and a plinth. They are painted with details in polychromy, with a gilt face and plaited beard, a rich collar, and three columns of inscription underneath, flanked by the four Sons of Horus and the goddesses Isis and Nephthys. Of course, the gilt face again stresses the divine status of the resurrected deceased.[293] Above, it has been noted that also the face of Djedhor's cartonnage was once gilt.[294] Hornedjitef's coffin has extensive decorations also on the inside,[295] in the case of Neswaiu and Takerheb these decorations are much simpler.

16.3. Hypocephalus

The decoration of the head of Djedhor's cartonnage includes a depiction of the winged scarab, an element which stresses its association with the rising sun and thereby helps in the resurrection of the mummy.[296] However, contemporary mummies were also given a magical aid to ensure their protection by the nocturnal sun in the netherworld. This idea was formulated in Chapter 162 of the Book of the Dead, a 'spell for providing heat under the head of the blessed one'.[297] Instead of 'heat' one should probably understand 'light' (the original term is *bs* 'flame').[298] This spell had 'to be said over a figure of the heavenly cow made of fine gold and placed at the throat of the corpse, or put into writing on a new sheet of papyrus placed under the head'.[299] It is this prescription which gave rise to the production of the so-called hypocephali: amuletic disks emulating the

287 PM I.2, 623–624; Quaegebeur 1995, 142; Walker/Bierbrier 1997, 29–30; Ikram/Dodson 1998, figs. 326–327; Strudwick 2006, 294–297; J.H. Taylor, in: Dawson/Strudwick 2016, 69 with fig. 44.

288 Lieblein 1868, 14–15, cat. 6–7; Schmidt 1919, 225 figs. 1298–1299; anonymous 1961, 114 cat. 167; van Hoeij 1998, 38–41.

289 Guidotti 2001, 40–42; Guidotti 2003.

290 For the design of their decoration, cf. Elias/Mekis 2019, 259. For the square heads, see already Ikram/Dodson 1998, 241, caption to figs. 326–327.

291 Cf. already Taylor 2002, 236, 241. For contemporary Ptah-Sokar-Osiris statues, see § 16.5 below.

292 Cf. Raven 1978–1979, 281–282.

293 Cf. n. 283 above.

294 See *supra*, § 7.1 and fig. 11.

295 Ikram/Dodson 1998, fig. 327.

296 *Supra* § 7.1. Cf. Hellinckx 2002, 202–203.

297 Allen 1974, 157, P 1.

298 Cf. the discussion in Mekis 2020, 78–80.

299 Allen 1974, 157, T 1.

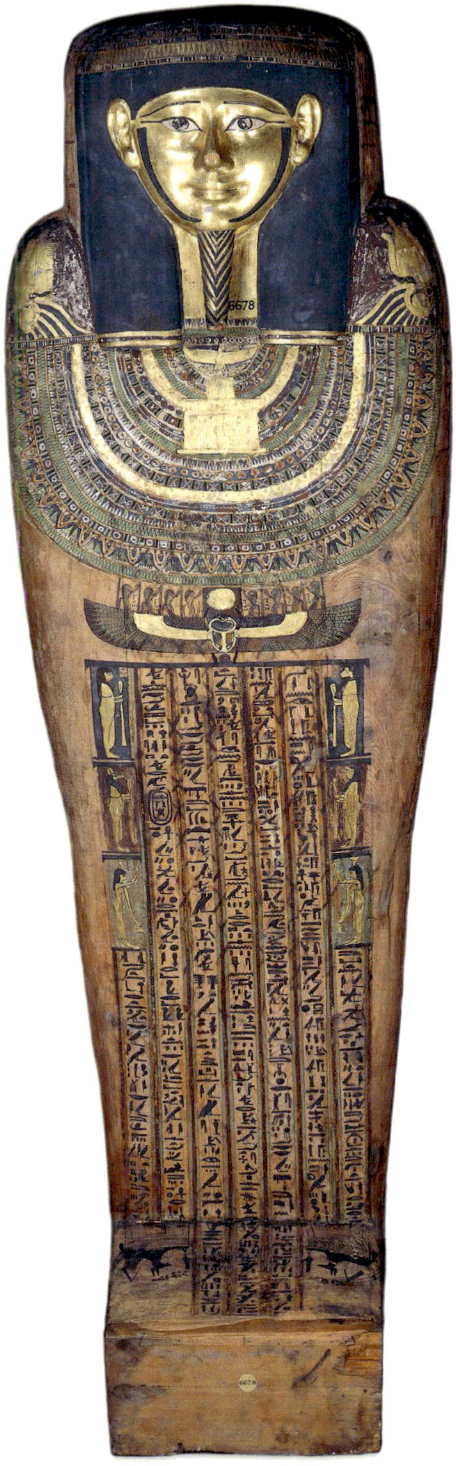

Fig. 49. Outer coffin of Hornedjitef (London, British Museum EA 6677. Image CC BY-NC-SA 4.0, © The Trustees of the British Museum).

Fig. 50. Inner coffin of Hornedjitef (London, British Museum EA 6678. Image CC BY-NC-SA 4.0, © The Trustees of the British Museum).

Fig. 53. Ptah-Sokar-Osiris figure of Hornedjitef (London, British Museum, EA 9736; Image CC BY-NC-SA 4.0, © The Trustees of the British Museum).

Ptah-Sokar-Osiris statues dating to the Ptolemaic Period usually belong to Type IV, which means they had either black or red bodies, gilt faces, and tall feather crowns.[317] This is indeed confirmed by the statues known from the burials of Djedhor's contemporaries which are being used here as reference material:

- Hornedjitef, London, British Museum, EA 9736 (Fig. 53).[318] The god has a blue wig, gilt face, ornamental collar, and a black body inscribed with a hymn in various columns of yellow hieroglyphs; the tall feather crown is now lost. Thus the statue can be recognized as a good example of type IVE.[319]
- Neswaiu, London, British Museum, EA 9737, still including its crown, type IVE.[320]
- Nestanetjeretten, Paris, Louvre, N 3508 E + N 3520 B, type IVE.[321]
- Paiuhor, Paris, Louvre, N 3520 A + N 2514 B, type IVE.[322]
- Nehemsyrattawy, Paris, Louvre, N 3510 E, base only.[323]

Thus, the members of the Theban elite which concern us here had a clear predilection for Ptah-Sokar-Osiris statues of type IVE. Obviously, such statues repeated the black-and-yellow colour scheme also visible in the outer coffins of their interments.

16.6. Stela

Presumably, Djedhor's funerary outfit also comprised a stela, an element which was rarely lacking from contemporary burials. Ever since the end of the New Kingdom, a time of anarchy when burials no longer included stone superstructures in order not to attract the attention of tomb robbers, the funerary stela was installed in the subterranean part of the tomb. Because it no longer had to withstand climatic conditions, it was generally made in painted wood, instead of the carved stone of former times. Such stelae occur in various different styles, each of them characteristic of a specific date and archaeological context.[324]

No stela is known for Djedhor. However, his contemporaries left a number of specimens which allow us to form a good impression of what his stela may have looked like:

- Neswaiu, London, British Museum, EA 8468 (Fig. 54).[325] This round-topped stela is of the lavish broad type mounted on two stepped supports and has a wooden *ba* bird on top. The decoration of the lunette shows a winged sun disk supported by a scarab, flanked by two winged uraei and two prostrated jackals. Below are two registers with Neswaiu adoring the solar barque, then the deceased worhipping a row of seven divinities, and finally an inscription in five lines. This stela is a good specimen of Munro's type 'Theben IV', a type which has been dated to the Ptolemaic Period.[326]
- Nestanetjeretten, Turin, Museo Egizio, C. 1599, a simpler version of the same type. Here the solar barque register has been omitted, while the adoration register has been replaced by an introduction scene: the deceased is led by Anubis to Osiris, Isis, Nephthys and Horus, whereas the inscription here counts no less than twelve lines.[327]
- Paiuhor, Turin, Museo Egizio, C. 1569, again has a simple version almost identical to the previous one but with ten lines of text.[328]

317 Raven 1978–1979, 266–271.
318 Quaegebeur 1995, 142; Strudwick 2006, 296–297.
319 Raven 1978–1979, 268.
320 Van Hoeij 1998, 33–36; Taylor 2001, fig. 156.
321 Mekis 2011, 51–56 and figs. 2–3.
322 Mekis 2011, 47 with n. 26, 53 with n. 41; Mekis 2019, 265–268.
323 Mekis 2011, 44 Doc. 10.
324 Cf. Munro 1973, 6–8.
325 PM I.2, 809; Munro 1973, 236; Bierbrier 1987, pls. 82–83; Van Hoeij 1998, 31–33; Taylor 2001, fig. 118.
326 Munro 1973, 43–50, 57–61.
327 Munro 1973, 244 and Abb. 73; Mekis 2011, 45–51 and fig. 1.
328 Munro 1973, 244 and Abb. 72; Mekis 2012, 263; Mekis 2019, 261–265.

Fig. 54. Stela of Neswaiu (London, British Museum, EA 8468; Image CC BY-NC-SA 4.0, © The Trustees of the British Museum).

PART III

DJEDHOR'S BURIAL AND ITS ARCHAEOLOGICAL CONTEXT

Fig. 55. Djedhor accompanied by the two Maʿat goddesses. Detail of Djedhor's Book of the Dead papyrus (RMO, inv. AL 61 vel 7).

Chapter 17

Date

The final paragraphs of Pleyte's *procès-verbal* represent an endeavour to date Djedhor's mummy.[329] Here he proposes a date around the transition from the XXVth to the XXVIth Dynasty, referring among others to the report by Birch on the Florence mummy. The latter, however, merely states that Takerheb's mummy must have been made after the expulsion of the Hyksos,[330] for no better reason than that two Asiatics are depicted on the footsoles of the cartonnage.[331] Pleyte himself adduces that the name of Djedhor's father, Neferibre, was the throne name of Psamtik II (595–589 BC), whereas a prince Djedhor would have been a son of that pharaoh. However, the first argument only gives a *terminus post quem*, and the second statement is incorrect.[332] Djedhor is rather the name of the second pharaoh of Dynasty XXX (365–360 BC), which might indicate another *terminus post quem*. Pleyte's remark that the occurrence of demotic likewise suggests a date from Dynasty XXVI onwards is of course correct. He also states that Djedhor's Book of the Dead papyrus is not unlike the Leiden papyri T 17 and T 18. Actually, T 17 is now dated to the Ptolemaic Period,[333] but T 18 is indeed a product of Dynasty XXVI.[334]

Pleyte also refers to a wooden stela of a woman Takerheb now in Leiden (cat. Leemans 1840, W 19; see Fig. 57), according to him likewise deriving from the Lescluze collection and therefore possibly from the same tomb as the Djedhor mummy. However, this stela does not have inventory number L.IX.8, as stated by Pleyte, but is numbered AH 21 and therefore stems from the Anastasi collection.[335] It mentions a woman Takerheb as the mother of the owner Pasheryenmin,[336] and therefore does not present any evidence that this person is related to Djedhor. However, the stela indeed comes from Thebes and has been dated to the middle to late Ptolemaic Period. At that time, the name Takerheb was rather common in Thebes (and elsewhere).[337] It should be noted that also the mother of Neswaiu was called Takerheb, though he had another father than Djedhor.[338]

Leemans (in his *Aanmerkingen*)[339] already questioned the Late Period date proposed by Pleyte, correctly arguing that the name Neferibre does not prove that Djedhor's father and king Psamtik II were contemporaries, and rather pointing to various Ptolemaic occurrences of these names. This accords rather well with the results of our survey of Djedhor's burial

---

329 *Supra*, Chapter 5, page 15 of the *procès-verbal*.
330 Birch 1855, 103.
331 Illustrated in Guidotti 2001, 42.
332 Cf. Dodson/Hilton 2004, 244 for what is known of the family of Psamtik II.
333 Quirke 1999, especially 37, 41–42, where a date around 130 BC is suggested. Cf. *supra*, n. 91.
334 Coenen 1999, 74.
335 Van Wijngaarden 1932, 2–4 no. 3 and pl. I. Cf. *supra*, ns. 92–93.
336 Cf. Munro 1973, 243.
337 Cf. De Meulenaere/Limme/Quaegebeur 1985, 63; Kákosy 1989, 118, figs. 136–137, 139–142; Van Hoeij 1998, 49 n. 72; Miatello 2008, 278.
338 Munro 1973, 236. Cf. Budge 1922, 138 with ill.; PM I.2, 809; Bierbrier 1987, pls. 82–83.
339 See *infra*, Appendix 1, note *g*.

goods in Chapters 7–16 above. There we have been able to draw the following chronological conclusions:

- The single-sheet or two-piece cartonnage is of a type which gradually developed in the course of the Ptolemaic Period, when the separate cartonnage pieces showed a tendeny to join together, and disappeared around the end of the 3rd century BC (Chapter 7).[340]
- The bead-net is of a specific type only known from a small number of Theban burials of Ptolemaic date (Chapter 9).[341]
- The crossed position of the mummy's arms is typical for Ptolemaic mummies (Chapter 15).[342]
- The gilded nails of Djedhor's mummy are characteristic of Dynasty XXX or the Ptolemaic Period (§ 11.3).[343]
- The padding of the mummy's breasts and the accentuation of the navel are phenomena recorded in a limited number of burials of the Ptolemaic and Roman Periods (§ 14.2 and 14.4).
- The Book of the Dead papyrus displays a well-known Ptolemaic style (§ 12.2).[344]
- The canopic box of Type C2 is datable to the Ptolemaic Period (§ 16.4).[345]
- Type IVE Ptah-Sokar-Osiris statues were in favour during Dynasty XXX and the Ptolemaic Period (§ 16.5).[346]

Moreover, the evidence presented above concerning some burials highly similar to Djedhor's now allows us to be much more precise. Most useful for dating purposes is the dossier of Hornedjitef, whose titles specify that he was a priest of the royal cult of the Euergetai (Ptolemy III and his Queen Berenike II), as well as of the King's mother Arsinoe II.[347] This allows us to date his burial ensemble between 246 and 221 BC.[348] As stated already by Quaegebeur, the Hornedjitef dossier provides a fixed date also for other contemporary material.[349] Both on the basis of the similarity of the archaeological material but also on genealogical evidence, the burials of Neswaiu, Takerheb, and Nestanetjeretten have all been dated slightly earlier, to the end of the 4th or the first half of the 3rd century BC,[350] and the same must be true for that of Djedhor. Paiuhor was probably buried together with Nestanetjeretten, a circumstance which led to the unvoluntary exchange of their cartonnage masks.[351]

340 Ikram/Dodson 1998, 187; Schreiber 2006; Mekis 2011; Mekis 2012, 249–250; Mekis 2019, 259; Raven 2024; Mekis, in: Wagner 2024, 257.

341 *Supra*, ns. 148 and 151.

342 *Supra*, n. 281.

343 *Supra*, n. 186.

344 *Supra*, n. 189.

345 *Supra*, n. 307.

346 Cf. Raven 1978–1979, 268–270; Raven 1980, 22–26.

347 Quaegebeur 1995, 143; cf. Strudwick 2006, 294.

348 Cf. Taylor 2001, 76, 87; Dawson/Strudwick 2016, 69.

349 Quaegebeur 1995, 161.

350 Neswaiu: Van Hoeij 1998, 44; http://collections.smvk.se/carlotta-mhm/web/object/3015853. Takerheb: Rosati 2003, 48; Rosati 2013, 6 with n. 22. Nestanetjeretten: Mekis 2011, 41 and 72.

351 Mekis 2012, 20–27; Mekis 2012, 251–253 and 267–269; Mekis 2019, 258, 260.

Chapter 18

Social status

18.1. Djedhor's titles

Some of Djedhor's funerary material is inscribed with a number of specific titles which suggest he belonged to the elite of contemporary Thebes. Foremost among these items is Djedhor's funerary papyrus, which mentions two important titles (Fig. 29):

- The first title given is that of 'high-priest of Khonsu, lord of lifetime' (*ḥm-nṯr n Ḫnsw nb ꜥḥꜥw*). This indicates that he belonged to the upper clergy of the local Khonsu temple, doubtless that of Karnak. The divine epithet 'lord of lifetime' is rather rare, but there are some other contemporary records of it, referring to Khonsu or other gods.[352] Khonsu *nb ꜥḥꜥw* is mainly attested in demotic documents only, whereas hieroglyphic texts use the epithet *ḥsb ꜥḥꜥw*. This may be just due to an orthographic confusion of the demotic.[353] It should be noted that this epithet seems to have led to the Greek name of the Karnak temple of Khonsu, Χεσβαιῆον.[354]
- The second title mentioned in the Book of the Dead papyrus is 'temple scribe' (*sš ḥwt-nṯr*), which seems to concern an administrative position in one of the Theban temples.
- One of the bandages of Djedhor's mummy specifies this position was held in the domain of Amun (*procès-verbal*, page 4, 46c fragment 19: *sš … n pr ꞽImn*).[355] Again this probably concerns the Karnak temple, where priests often combined offices in the various separate sanctuaries.
- Less certain are the inscriptions written on other mummy bandages, which are hardly legible in places but seem to contain a number of additional titles. One title seems to concern a priestly function connected with the tutelary deity of Upper Egypt, Nekhbet (*procès-verbal*, 46c fragments 19, 21–22: Fig. 22, second bandage): *sš (-nsw) n pr Nḫb.t nṯr.t … n mn …* Although Pleyte wanted to read the name of Wadjet (patron of Lower Egypt) as well, it is more probable that the name of Nekhbet is followed by an epithet of some kind, starting with *nṯr.t*.
- The same bandage also mentions the title 'royal scribe' (*sš nsw*), or *basilikos grammateus* according to the Greek administration of Ptolemaic Egypt.[356] The title is written twice, a dittography which may be a confusion caused by the following title 'scribe of the domain of Amun …'.[357]

352 Coenen 1999, 75; Leitz 2002, III.604.
353 De Meulenaere 1998, 1128.
354 *Ibid.*, 1128–1130.
355 This is read by Petra Hogenboom as *sš n pr ꞽImn n pr* […], implying that another temple was mentioned as well. Cf. Birk 2020, 208–210.
356 Cf. Rosati 2013, 221. For the title, see Hölbl 2001, 59 with n. 128; Birk 2020, 209.
357 I thank Petra Hogenboom for her study of the titles on the linen bandages.

18.2. Djedhor's parentage

Djedhor's bandages state that he inherited his titles from his father, who is called *mỉ-nn* 'ditto'. Djedhor's father is mentioned on various objects from his burial and was called Neferibre.[358] As we have seen in Chapter 17, Pleyte already signaled this man was named after Pharaoh Psamtik II. Numerous inscriptions on Djedhor's funerary items also give his mother's name, Takerheb. Leemans, in his *Aanmerkingen*, appears to have been the first to suggest that this Takerheb was none other than the owner of the burial ensemble and mummy now in Florence.[359] He writes:

> 'Remarkable is the similarity in a number of peculiarities of the mummy of Saho [= Djedhor, MJR] in the Leiden Museum with the mummy of a Takarheb, daughter of Aahpehpeh and Nebtenhi, in the Museum at Florence, unwrapped and described by Prof Migliarini in 1827. The report written by him in Italian was translated in English and included, together with annotations by S. Birch, in *Archaeologia* vol. XXXVI.1855 pp. 161ff. Both mummies seem to belong to the same period. Takerhib in the Florence Museum may have been the mother of Saho in the Museum in Leiden, and thus married to Nefer-ra-ab.'

I myself have accepted this theory about the mother-son relationship in the past,[360] but perhaps we should be more cautious. The name Takerheb was very common at the time, at least in Theban priestly circles.[361] The names of the parents of the Florence mummy, Aapehty and Nebetdenehyt, are not instructive on this matter. All we can say is that the name Takerheb may (or may not) be an indication of family ties. It should be noted that also Neswaiu in Stockholm had a mother called Takerheb, but his father was a certain Tjaimu and therefore he cannot have been a full brother of Djedhor.

18.3. Djedhor's social circles

The titles of Djedhor and his father Neferibre make an interesting comparison with the titulary present on the comparative burial material of other individuals used in the preceding chapters:

- Takerheb in Florence was the daughter of a royal scribe and high-priest.[362]
- The cartonnage of Horemheb in the British Museum mentions no titles.
- Neswaiu in Stockholm was a temple scribe in the 2nd phyle of Montu, doubtless again in Karnak.[363]
- Nestanetjeretten was only a sistrum-player of Amun-Re in Karnak, like her mother, but she stemmed from a family of god's fathers of that sanctuary and was married to another priest of that rank.[364]
- Paiuhor was yet another god's father and high-priest of the cult of Amun at Karnak, but also served as temple scribe of Amun and *wab*-priest in the temple of Mut.[365]
- Hornedjitef in London was certainly the most prominent member of the sacerdotal group that concerns us here: apart from being a god's father and high-priest of Amun in Karnak, he also held a great number of other sacerdotal offices.[366]

All this indicates that this specific kind of elite burials was especially reserved for the circles of the upper clergy of the Karnak temples. These were people of great social standing[367] and some of them also erected public monuments for themselves on the grounds of the Karnak temple.[368] Djedhor, however, has so far almost escaped the attention of the specialists of this historical period. There is an entry in the *Prosopographia Ptolemaica* devoted to a Djedhor son of Takerheb,[369] and referring to a Book of the Dead papyrus in the Louvre (N 3128), but in this case the father's name seems to be Wahibre (Apries)[370] so it must concern another person (though perhaps a family member).[371] No statues of his seem to be known either.

The fact that the members of a specific social circle would have had an exclusive tradition of burial is in itself nothing unusual. These sets of burial goods may be described as forming an archaeological assemblage: an associated set of contemporary artefact-types.[372] Similar assemblages

358 Cf. Coenen 1999, 75.

359 *Infra*, Appendix 1, page 3.

360 Raven 1993, 66; Raven/Taconis 2005, 30. Also accepted by Guidotti 2009, 22.

361 See n. 337 above.

362 Guidotti 2001, 40 and ill. on page 41 (coffin); Mekis 2020, 219–220, no. 74; cf. Birch 1855, pl. XV.

363 Van Hoeij 1998, 28.

364 Mekis 2011, 41–45; Mekis 2020, 218–219, no. 73.

365 Mekis 2012, 263–264; Mekis 2019, 260; Mekis 2020, 198–199, no. 50.

366 Quaegebeur 1995, 143–144; Mekis 2020, 236, no. 96.

367 As such, they deserve their entries in the *Prosopographia Ptolemaica* (Peremans/Van 't Dack 1907–1986): Hornedjitef: PP III, 5459, 5649, 7257; Nestanetjeretten: PP IX, 7112c; Paiuhor: PP IX, 5775j.

368 Neswaiu: see Van Hoeij 1998, 22–31 (coll. Six); Nestanetjeretten's son Nesmin: see Mekis 2011, 44 Doc. 11 (Cairo JE 37017). Cf. Raven 1980, 21–22 Docs. A–C for another contemporary family of Karnak priests known both from public monuments and funerary goods.

369 PP IX.5841a: *Teos f. de Tkalibis.*

370 Champollion 2013, 132 with ill.

371 For this person, see Coenen 1999, 71–73 (the other half of his Book of the Dead ended up in Leiden, inv. AMS 47a).

372 Cf. Clarke 1978, 489.

of archaeological material have been recognized before as manifestations of distinct subcultures. In the present case, because of their association with the members of the Theban clergy of the (first half of the) Ptolemaic Period, we may speak of both a regional subculture as an occupational subculture.[373] The occurrence of a limited amount of internal variation – for instance in the types of stela or hypocephalus concerned – is only to be expected, since an assemblage is only a polythetic set of different artefact-types repeatedly found together.[374] Thus, the existence of such variations would still have allowed members of contemporary society to immediately recognize the exclusive character of the burial goods involved. Such exclusivity was an appropriate reflection of the privileged social position which these sacerdotal individuals held in Ptolemaic Egypt, where the Greek rulers and the native clergy preserved a careful balance in an endeavour to keep the country quiet and to earn the loyalty of Egypt's population.[375] High-ranking priests from all parts of the country used to be summoned to the royal court once a year for a discussion of matters concerning the temples and the cult. This association with the ruler, alone, would already have distinguished the priests in question from the rest of the native population.

A further factor which set apart the sacerdotal ranks would have been the circumstance that they spent their life in a segment of society that remained closed to others, and that they had to be purified and initiated before they could enter the consecrated part of the temple in order to perform their duties. This also explains the fact that priestly offices were often inherited from father to son. Finally, because of their training and special education they would have developed a predilection for specific ceremonies and attributes that were lacking from the funerary ritual of their contemporaries. Thus, we have observed above how for instance the occurrence of a hypocephalus was apparently restricted to priestly burials,[376] and the same seems to be true for the Type IVE Ptah-Sokar-Osiris statues and the wooden stelae of the type 'Theben IV'.[377] Moreover, in the specific attributes suggesting a *Gliedervergottung* and a unification with the demiurge, these burials seem to express a clear fascination for esoteric themes that one does not encounter in contemporary interments of other classes of society.

373 For the terminology and its implications, see Clarke 1978, 249–261.
374 Clarke 1978, 250.
375 Cf. Hölbl 2001, 105–111, 279–285.
376 *Supra* § 16.3 with n. 300.
377 Cf. Raven 1978–1979, 268–270; Raven 1980, 22–26; Munro 1973, 235–245.

Chapter 19

Provenance

19.1. Hornedjitef

In the sale's catalogue of the De Lescluze collection, no provenance is given for the mummy and cartonnage of Djedhor (Fig. 9).[378] The Theban origin of this burial ensemble readily transpires from Djedhor's titles inscribed on the various items, especially his sacerdotal offices in the temples of Amun and Khonsu.[379] However, it is possible to be more precise by taking into account what is known about the findspot of the other funerary finds discussed above as comparative material. Thus it has been recorded that the objects of Hornedjitef (cf. Figs. 17, 49–51, 53, 56) were found in a tomb beside the causeways of the Deir el-Bahari temples, probably in the area of large Late Period tombs in el-Assasif, some of which seem to have been reused in this period.[380] Recently, some remains found in the tomb of Ibi (TT 36, indeed situated in the said area next to the causeway of Hatshepsut) were identified as belonging to two sisters of Hornedjitef.[381] This might indicate that also Hornedjitef was once interred there as a secondary burial. The find was made by Giovanni d'Athanasi in the 1820s, and the whole set (except for the canopic box) was acquired by the British Museum at the auction of the collection of the British consul-general Henry Salt in 1835.[382] The box had by then already ended up in Leiden in 1829, as part of the collection of the Swedish consul-general, Giovanni d'Anastasi (Fig. 56).[383] This reflects the custom of 19th-century dealers and explorers to share spectacular finds with others. In this specific case, the Greek explorer Athanasi (who worked for Salt in Thebes and lived in a house close to TT 52 in Sheikh Abd el-Qurneh, the famous tomb of Nakht), may have sold the box to the Italian dealer Piccinini, who acted as the local agent for Anastasi.[384]

Nothing seems to be known about the provenance of the mummy and cartonnage of Horemheb, now in the British Museum, except that these were also bought from Salt in 1835 and may therefore be from the same location.

378 Anonymous 1826, 35, no. L.XII.2. For the sale, see above, Chapter 3.

379 See above, § 18.1.

380 PM I.2, 623–624; Strudwick/Taylor 2003, 162, 174 with fig. 3.

381 T. Mekis, in: Wagner 2024, 256. I owe this reference to T. Mekis.

382 Walker/Bierbrier 1997, 29–30. For Athanasi and Salt, see Bierbrier 2019, 23–24 and 409–410. See D'Athanasi 1836, 75–77 with cat. 852.

383 Inv.no. AH 215. For Anastasi, see Bierbrier 2019, 16.

384 For Athanasi's house, see C. Simpson, in: Strudwick/Taylor 2003, 247 and pls. 145–146. For Piccinini, see Bierbrier 2019, 366. A new study of Piccinini and his activities as an art dealer is in preparation by Eva Cornelisse; see www.academia.edu/106362695/Traces_of_Piccinini.

Fig. 56. Canopic box of Hornedjitef (RMO, inv. AH 215).

19.2. Neswaiu

Piccinini had a house near the south end of the nearby necropolis of Dra Abu 'n-Naga, close to tomb 161 (of another Nakht).[385] This may have put him in the position to play an important role in the exploration of further Ptolemaic tombs in that area. At least, it has been recorded by the British scholar John Gardner Wilkinson that the findspot of Neswaiu's burial was located 'in the hill of Piccinini's house'.[386] Neswaiu's coffins and mummy were duly delivered to Piccinini's patron, Anastasi, who donated them to Karl XIV Johan, King of Sweden, in 1826 (cf. Fig. 18).[387] The set was displayed in the Stockholm Royal Palace, then transferred to the National Museum in the 1860s and from there to the Medelhavsmuseet (the present-day Världskulturmuseerna) in 1928.[388] Yet, Anastasi kept Neswaiu's stela for himself until 1839, when it was sold to the British Museum (Fig. 54); the same may have happened with the Ptah-Sokar-Osiris figure, which is now in the same collection but without known pedigree.

Finally, we may add that the cartonnage of Ankhefenkhonsu was found in the 1970s in TT 157 (of Nebwenenef), likewise in Dra Abu 'n-Naga, during excavations by the Pennsylvania Museum.[389] This tomb lies a bit uphill from Piccinini's house.

19.3. Nestanetjeretten and Nehemsyrattawy

The burial goods of Nestanetjeretten likewise seem to have come from Dra Abu 'n-Naga.[390] It has been assumed that she was buried together with her daughter Nehemsyrattawy. The latter's hypocephalus was found by Clarence Fisher in 1921 during an expedition in that necropolis,[391] but her other goods (now dispersed over the Avignon Musée Calvet and the Louvre) were acquired early in the 19th century.[392] Nestanetjeretten's own funerary outfit consists of the above-mentioned cartonnage in the Louvre, a stela in Turin (C. 1599), a Ptah-Sokar-Osiris figure (Louvre N 3508 E + 3520 B), a hypocephalus (Turin C. 2324,) and a Book of the Dead papyrus (Vatican 38609). The latter was acquired around 1820,[393] the Turin objects before 1882, the Louvre figure before 1857.[394] The cartonnage was bought or excavated by Alexander Rhind in Luxor between 1855 and 1857, and arrived in Paris via Edinburgh and Lyon.[395]

19.4. Paiuhor

It is remarkable that the mask of Nestanetjeretten's cartonnage bears an inscription for Paiuhor, who was probably buried in the same tomb and whose mask bears an inscription for Nehemsyrattawy.[396] This appears to be a stupid mistake by the ancient scribe; the two masks cannot have been interchanged during their peregrinations on the art market, since Nestanetjeretten's cartonnage has a fixed mask and is of the one-piece type. Paiuhor's specimen was likewise acquired via the collections of Rhind, who must have acquired the two cartonnages during his stay in Luxor in the years 1855–1857. It is well-known he did some excavations himself at the foot of Sheikh Abd el-Qurneh and at el-Assasif, but he does not appear to mention these cartonnages explicitly in his report.[397]

19.5. Takerheb

Other explorers were also around to share in the promising Ptolemaic finds. Thus the mummy and coffins of Takerheb, which were acquired by the Grand Duke of Tuscany, Ferdinando III, in 1824, were bought from Gilbert Courbarien, a tailor in Alexandria who is also known as a collaborator of the French consul-general Bernardino Drovetti.[398] It was not until 1884 that they ended up in the Archaeological Museum of Florence. Drovetti was not exactly on peaceful terms with the men of Henry Salt, so that we may infer that Takerheb was perhaps buried at some distance from Neswaiu and Hornedjitef. Though it is very tricky to define the exact spheres of influence of the various dealers at the time, we may have indications of where to look in this particular case.

Thus a ceiling of TT 32 (of Djehutymes) still bears an incised signature of Drovetti's assistant Antonio Lebolo.[399]

385 See C. Simpson, in: Strudwick/Taylor 2003, 247 and fig. 1.

386 PM I.2, 832. For Wilkinson, see Bierbrier 2019, 491–493. For his house in Sheikh Abd el-Qurneh (near TT 83 according to PM I.1, 493), see C. Simpson, in: Strudwick/Taylor 2003, 247 with pl. 137.

387 Van Hoeij 1998, 44.

388 I thank Sofia Häggman for the acquisition information.

389 Mekis 2011, 58 n. 49. For the cartonnage, see *supra*, n. 119.

390 For the following, see Mekis 2011, 43–44; Mekis 2019, 258ff.

391 Apparently near TT 305–307: see PM I.2, 610–611 (now Philadelphia 29.86.436). This is downhill from the main cemetery, so perhaps the hypocephalus just fell down a shaft there as a result of pillaging.

392 The Ptah-Sokar-Osiris figure (Louvre N 3510 E) was acquired with the Salt collection in 1826: Mekis 2011, 44 Doc. 10. The Book of the Dead (Louvre N 3149 + N 3204 B) was acquired before 1857 (Champollion 2013, 68: N = registre Napoléon III). The Avignon cartonnage fragment (Musée Calvet A 67A) was acquired in 1842 (Cavalier 2011, 68, Cat. 19).

393 Mekis 2011, 67.

394 Cf. Champollion 2013, 68 (and see n. 392 above).

395 Mekis 2011, 57. For Rhind, see Bierbrier 2019, 391–392.

396 Mekis 2012, 251–253 and 267–269.

397 Rhind 2002, Chapters IV and V.

398 Rosati 2013, 216–217 (refuting the previous mention of a certain 'Giberti' as the seller of these items). For Drovetti, see Bierbrier 2019, 136.

399 For Lebolo, see Bierbrier 2019, 268. For his signature, see Kákosy 1989, 86 no. II, cf. also 118; Kákosy *et al.* 2004, 337 and pl. LXXVI.

This tomb is situated in el-Khokha, opposite Dra Abu 'n-Naga across the entrance to Deir el-Bahari and not far from el-Assasif. It is quite clear that Drovetti's men did extensive work in that particular tomb, and various objects from Djehutymes's burial have ended up in the Turin Museum, which bought Drovetti's first collection in 1824.[400] Among these acquisitions may have been the cartonnages C. 2257 and C. 2258; the latter is certainly from the Drovetti collection,[401] though the museum records merely state the former was acquired before 1882.[402] But we have further indications that cartonnages of this particular type have been found in TT 32 during recent excavations.[403] These belonged to various members of the family of Nesmin, high-priest of Amun-Re.[404] The excavations in TT 32 also produced various fragments of linen highly similar to those retrieved from the mummies of Djedhor and Takerheb.[405]

19.6. Djedhor

All this suggests that the burial ensemble of Djedhor (about which nothing has been recorded) must also have been found in the archaeological zone extending from el-Khokha over el-Assasif to the centre of the hill of Dra Abu 'n-Naga. In fact, in recent research this whole area has been recognized as one vast Ptolemaic cemetery.[406] Some of the Ptolemaic priests attached to the Karnak temples installed their burials in pre-existing rock-tombs of earlier date, others constructed simple mud-brick complexes especially in el-Assasif.[407] We have no date for the discovery of Djedhor's funerary goods either, but can infer that it must have taken place around the same period as those of the other burials discussed above. The mummy and cartonnage (Figs. 13–16) were bought from De Lescluze in 1826, who himself had acquired them in Alexandria two years earlier, probably from François Barthou.[408] This dealer acted as an intermediary between the Dutch government and Anastasi during the sale of the latter's collections in 1828, but he was also in touch with Drovetti, Salt, and other contemporary diplomats/dealers, as has recently been established in a survey of De Lescluze's collection.[409] Thus, he may just have shared in their discoveries in the Theban area. The same is suggested by the other objects inscribed for Djedhor and now in the Louvre: his canopic chest (N 2644, Fig. 52) and a part of his Ptah-Sokar-Osiris figure (AF 708).[410] Both came from the collection Edmé Antoine Durand in 1825.[411] It is known that Durand was in Turin in that same year, when the Salt collection was on offer in Leghorn. The bead net in the Louvre, possibly from Djedhor's burial, was acquired with the Salt collection in 1826 (inv. N 3078, Fig. 21).[412] Possibly, this means that Djedhor's burial was originally discovered by Salt before 1824, but in view of the frequent exchanges of objects between the various dealers this must remain unclear.

400 Kákosy 1989, figs. 111–112.
401 Donadoni-Roveri 1988, 232 no. 321.
402 See www.collezioni.museoegizio.it.
403 Mekis 2011, 59 n. 50.
404 Mekis 2011, 58–59.
405 Kákosy 1989, figs. 53–56, 60; Schreiber 2007.
406 Cf. Strudwick/Taylor 2003, 171–176, 183 fig. 8.
407 Strudwick/Taylor 2003, 172–173 and fig. 3 (marked 'MMA 1915–16' and 'Carnarvon excavations').
408 For Barthou, see Bierbrier 2019, 38. For the acquisition, see Raven, in: Ter Keurs/Wirtz 2018, 69.
409 Raven, in: Ter Keurs/Wirtz 2018, 70–71.
410 See Champollion 2013, 288–289, cat.no. R.7 with ill. N 2644; 312, cat. U 1.
411 For Durand, see *ibid.*, 28, 30; Bierbrier 2019, 140.
412 Cf. Chapter 9 above.

Chapter 20

Conclusion

The uncontrolled excavation of Djedhor's tomb and the dispersal of his funerary items at the beginning of the 19th century, followed by the final destruction of his mummy due to the 1878 autopsy, represent irreparable losses that seriously hamper our understanding of this extraordinary find. Yet a careful study of Pleyte's *procès-verbal* and a scrutinous comparison of Djedhor's mummy trappings with parallels in other museums can do much to repair the damages and to reconstruct the original burial ensemble. Thus it is now clear that the mummy was buried according to the highest standards of early Ptolemaic burials in Thebes – burials which were apparently reserved for the local priests of the Karnak sanctuary. Originally, the burial must have consisted of the following items:

- an exterior mummiform coffin, painted in black with details in yellow (lost);
- an inner coffin with details in polychromy and gold leaf (lost);
- a cartonnage covering the mummy's front and sides, all in polychromy with gilt details (Leiden inv. L.XII.2-d, damaged with rear of head-end completely lost, Figs. 13–16);
- a bead net with various motifs along the upper border in mosaic work (possibly Louvre inv. N. 3078, Fig. 21);
- a hypocephalus (lost);
- a mummy with manifold attributes, such as an amuletic necklace (Fig. 31), a Book of the Dead papyrus (Figs. 28–29), various decorated shrouds, etc. (mummy destroyed during autopsy, but attributes preserved in Leiden, inv. AL 1–64 and L.XII.2);
- a canopic box (Louvre inv. N 2644, Fig. 52);
- a Ptah-Sokar-Osiris statue (Louvre inv. AF 708, now deposited in Lille);
- and presumably a wooden stela (lost).

Thanks to the *procès-verbal* by Pleyte of the autopsy which he executed in 1878, we are able to visualise the original appearance of Djedhor's mummy. This document has been kept in the archives of the Leiden Museum of Antiquities, which also preserves the numerous attributes and samples taken from the mummy on that occasion. However, it is the comparison of these items which similar burials of the same period which help us understanding Djedhor's wealth and social position. This is corroborated by his titles, which had never before been studied in detail. Djedhor officiated as a high-priest in the cult of Khonsu, 'lord of lifetime', in the Karnak temple devoted to this moon-god. He combined this office with that of a temple scribe in the sanctuary of Amun next-door, and apparently held some office in the cult of the tutelary goddess of Upper Egypt, Nekhbet. Besides, he acted as 'royal scribe', the equivalent of the Greek title *basilikos grammateus*, which meant he was involved in the local administration of estates and land on behalf of the Greek government. He probably spent his whole life within the temple complex at present-day Karnak.

Moreover, this 'second autopsy' of the remaining documentation enables us to roughly reconstruct the location of the findspot of Djedhor's burial. Clearly, it was situated in the Theban necropolis, between el-Khokha and Dra Abu 'n-Naga, where the Ptolemaic priests attached to the Karnak temples had their own private cemetery. Apparently, Djedhor's burial was retrieved around 1820 by the native explorers working for the European diplomats residing in Alexandria, or by the agents of these Europeans living in houses strategically located in the ancient necropolis. At the moment of its discovery, Djedhor's funerary ensemble had already suffered from decay or previous robberies. This explains that certain items have been lost, others (such as the coffin) were replaced by objects from other interments, and some objects had sustained damage (such as the cartonnage). Then the discoverers added to the confusion by splitting up the various items and offering them for sale to different collectors. As a result of this, Djedhor's objects have been dispersed over various collections, including at least the Leiden Museum and the Louvre. It cannot be excluded that more of his funerary possessions will turn up in other places in the future.

Regarding the family ties of Djedhor, we can assume he was related to some of the other priests of the Karnak temples. It is certain that he inherited most of his titles from his father Neferibre. However, we do not feel so sure any longer about the assumption that his mother's mummy and coffin are now in Florence. The name Takerheb is very common in the Ptolemaic Period, and keeps turning up in the circles of the Karnak priests. All we can say is that both individuals (Djedhor and the Florence Takerheb) were embalmed and buried in the same way and probably at the same period. Unfortunately, the destruction of both mummies during the 19th-century dissections means no modern genetic typing can be performed on human tissue of both individuals, in order to prove or disprove that they were mother and son.[413] If they were in fact related, we cannot exclude the possibility that they once shared a common tomb in western Thebes. For the moment, we can only confirm that the two burials were discovered almost simultaneously, shortly before the year 1824 when Takerheb's burial was sold by Courbarien to Ferdinando III of Tuscany, and Djedhor's by Barthou to De Lescluze.

Above, reference has already been made to the increasing awareness of the ethical aspects involved in the way how museums should deal with human remains, especially when such relics derive from non-western cultures. The pillage of Djedhor's burial, the sale of his funerary items and his mortal remains, then the dispersion of the various items over several different locations, and finally the destructive manner in which his mummy was investigated – all these acts can be qualified as interventions that clash with the Ancient Egyptian expectations of an eternal existence in the hereafter. Moreover, the fact that nothing had been done to publish the scientific data gained from this violent behaviour can be regarded as a further blemish. Let us hope that the above reconstruction of the interment of this forgotten Ptolemaic priest (although a reconstruction on paper only) will at least offer some compensation for what was committed in the Theban necropolis 200 years ago, and that it will help the spirit of Djedhor, the son of Neferibre and Takerheb, to find some peace in the realm of Osiris. From now onwards, at least his name will survive in the scientific records.

413 Of Takerheb, some mummy tissue remains in Florence (personal communication by Anna Consonni).

Appendix 1

Comments by Leemans (*Aanmerkingen* = Archives RMO, box C93, 6.4.3/3 *sub* 2.1.1)

Translated from the Dutch. Texts in italics are underlined in the original.

[Page 1]

Comments on the *report* regarding the investigation of a Mummy from the *de l'Escluze* sale at Antwerp (*Catalogue / Description raisonnée* M 46, 47) of the Aegypt. Monum.[414]

P. 1 (*a*) Mummy and appurtenances have not been bought at the 1826 sale in Antwerp, but were withheld by the seller; purchased from him by the Museum at a later stage, in March 1827, together with other withheld pieces.[415]

(*b*) Dash? What does that mean?

(*c*) When the mummy with the coffins was received by the Museum, the so-called *cardboard coffin* (originally just an ordinary inner coffin manufactured from linen and stucco, or plaster, designated as *Cartonnage de momie* by Champollion) was in a most lacunary condition, certainly not forming a coherent whole, but rather anything but an entire object.

(*d*) The preliminary investigation by Reuvens was only restricted to collecting the smaller objects lying loose with the mummy etc.: *beads*, fragments of the *network leaves*, *linen bandages*, etc.

This comment should also be kept in mind at the end of p. 5, which again refers to an investigation by Reuvens; likewise at the beginning of p. 6.

P. 2 (*e*) In 1840, the so-called cardboard coffin was roughly in the same condition as in 1827, though the *gilt mask*, apparently completely missing *now*, was probably damaged rather more. Accordingly, this mask is not separately mentioned in my description.

I do not know what is meant by the *découpures* of the *de l'Escluze Catalogue*; the word signifies: *cut-out ornament*; perhaps they refer to the *figures découpées à jour*. The *cartonnage* was originally laced up at the rear, probably like this:[416]

The *loose* bandages or wrappings with inscriptions had been deposited by Reuvens in a wooden box, closed by means of a sheet of glass glued on top.

---

414 This abbreviation refers to the *Monumens égyptiens* (Leemans 1839–1905), published both in French and in Dutch. These lithographic folio plates can be understood as the illustrations belonging to Leemans's catalogue *Description raisonnée* (Leemans 1840), with which they share the same subdivision and numbering system. See Raven 1992, 11.

415 This is clearly incorrect, as explained *supra* in n. 52.

416 Likewise incorrect, see *supra*, § 7.1 with ns. 98–99.

[Page 2]

P. 3 (*f*) Mummy of *Thar* son of *Kerheb*.

Thar (*Tsathar*, *Tather*), but I think during the period to which the deceased seems to belong one should retain the lecture or pronunciation *Tsa ho*, *Saho*, or *Tsjaho*.  is transcribed on the Graeco-Egyptian coffins, for instance that of ΣΕΝΣΑΩΣ, 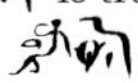 as ΣΑΩΣ , the final Σ is a Greek ending.[417] *Brugsch* made a grave mistake when he rendered Σενσαώς as *T-se-n-aäh, daughter of the moon*, in his *Samml. dem. griech. Eigennamen*.[418]

Τεώς (according to Syncellus, Manetho, Africanus, etc.), also Ταχώς (according to *Diodorus* and others, various spellings of the name of the 2nd king of the XXXth dynasty, 360 BC) are probably Greek transcriptions of the same or similar 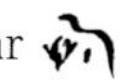 , where the χ in Ταχώς can represent the ϩο or ϩω (cf. Copt. ϫω), only with a more pronounced aspiration.

P. 5 (*g*) I still have some doubts concerning the period to which the mummy has to belong.

P. 15 (*g*)Our *Tsaho*, *Taho*, or *Sao* may have lived during the first kings of the Ptolemaic Period. I would date to the same period the wooden stela in the Museum, marked W.19, of *Psenpa*, the son of *Psenχem* and *Takerhib*, because of the style and the shape of the hieroglyphs.[419]

That the father of our *Saho* is called *Nefer-ab-ra* (*Nefer-ra-ab*), which name is identical to that of the second cartouche of Psamtik II of the XXVIth dynasty, certainly does not *prove* that our deceased belongs to the time of that dynasty. In the Ptolemaic Period a priest of Ptah-Sokar-Osiris had the same name *Ra-nefer-ab* (*Nefer-ab-ra*); he was the father of a priestess and princess *Philotera-har-saônkh*. A certain *Philotera* is mentioned as a sister of *Ptolemy Philadelphos II* (and of *Antinoe II*);[420] however, I do not know whether she is identical to the above-mentioned one, with *har-sa-ônkh* being added to *Philotera*.

It occurs very frequently that a royal name without further additions

[Page 3]

was used as the personal name of a non-royal person, but the thus-named person does not necessarily have to be dated to the reign of that king. The above-mentioned *Nefer-ab-ra* lived several centuries after *Psamtik II*.

Remarkable is the similarity in a number of peculiarities of the mummy of *Saho* in the Leiden Museum with the mummy of a certain *Takarheb*, daughter of *Aahpehpeh* and *Neb.tenhi*, in the Museum at Florence, unwrapped and described by Prof. Migliarini in 1827. The report written by him in Italian was translated in English and included, together with annotations by S. Birch, in *Archaeologia* vol. XXXVI.1855 pp. 161ff.[421] Both mummies seem to belong to the same period. *Takerhib* in the Florence Museum may have been the mother of *Saho* in the Museum in Leiden, and thus married to *Nefer-ra-ab*. Otherwise I regard the *Ta* of the name of this woman as an integral element of her name, and thereby accuse the Egyptian scribe of neglect or impetuosity where this syllable is missing.[422]

The style of handwriting does not plead against the opinion that our *Saho* might go back to the period of the Psamtiks, though a comparison with hieratic script

417 This refers to the coffin of Sensaos, RMO inv.no. AMM 8. Cf. Raven/Taconis 2005, cat. 26 with ref.

418 The reference is to Brugsch 1851, 36.

419 For this stela, cf. *supra*, ns. 92–93. See *infra*, Fig. 57.

420 For Philotera, see Hölbl 2001, 24, 103 and 354–355 (Stemma 1). Cf. *ibid.*, 103 with n. 160, for Heresankh, priestess of the deified Philotera and herself a member of the family of the Memphite high-priests.

421 For the mummy of Takerheb, daughter of Aapehty and Nebetdenehyt, see Birch 1855.

422 This verdict is a bit too strict; cf. *infra*, n. 428 with references, which clearly state that Kerheb (without initial Ta-) is just a variant.

of the first Ptolemaic centuries should produce additional data. Such texts make mention of a *Saho* (*Tsaho*), priest of Phtah and Amen-Ra, son of *Petekahen* and the woman *Tasje-ra-he*, and another *Saho*, son of *Pe-tep-monχ* and of the woman *Mempe-nofre*, priest of *Imhotep*;[423] but it remains to be assessed to which period *those Saho's* belong.

I certainly do not deny the pronunciation *Thar* or *har* of 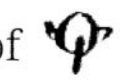, but for *these* proper names I cannot

[Page 4]

accept it. This comment is also relevant for p. 4 lines 6 and 2 from below in the *report*, and elsewhere.

Leiden, July 4, 1878 [signed] C. Leemans

423 These are the owners of the Louvre sarcophagi D 8 and D 9 (see https://collections.louvre.fr/en/ark:/53355/cl010036401 and /cl010037229), althouh the parents' names have been garbled. In fact, the names should be read as Djedhor, son of Padiheka and Tasheryt(en)taihet (D 8) and Djedhor, son of Padimenekh and Neferrenpet (D 9).

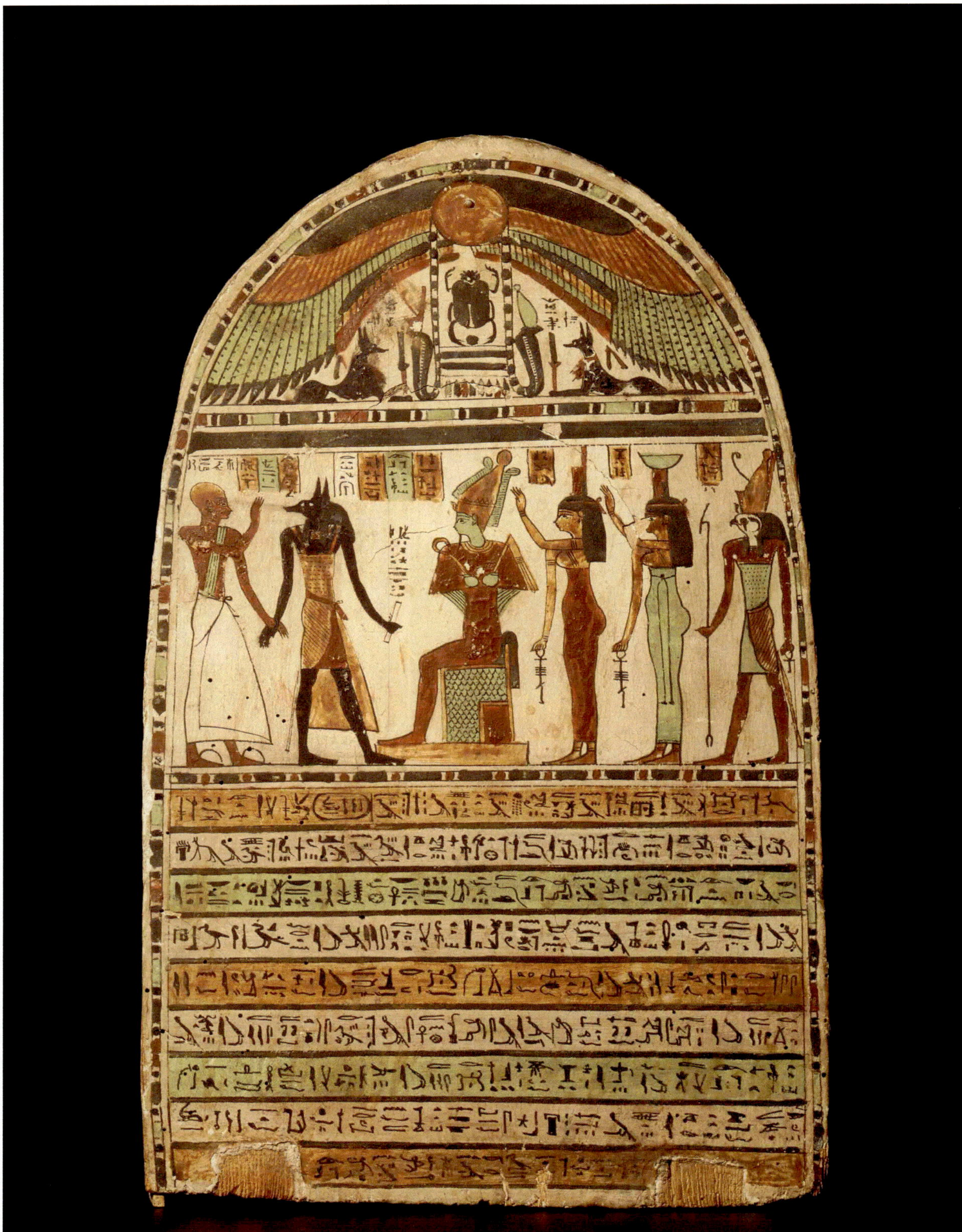

Fig. 57. Wooden stela of Pasheryenmin (RMO, inv. AH 21 = cat. Leemans 1840, W 19).

Appendix 2

Reply by Pleyte (*Opmerkingen* = Archives RMO, box C93, 6.4.3/3 *sub* 2.1.1).

Translated from the Dutch.

[Page 1]
Annotations
regarding the comments on the report dealing with the investigation of the Mummy M.46, 47.

(a) Very true. This comment is written on the first page of the Catalogue in the hand of Prof. Reuvens.[424]

(b) Reuvens has collected the paragraphs by means of lines in red chalk, both those referring to the linen wrappings or the cardboard coffin, and those regarding the wooden coffin.[425]

(c) [no comments]

(d) There is a marked difference between the present condition of the Mummy and that described in the Catalogue *de l'Escluze*. The cartonnage was then completely open, or only the face or gold mask was *un peu écrasée*. If Reuvens did not investigate the Mummy, it must have been investigated before he purchased it in 1827, otherwise it has been incorrectly described in the Catalogue. Moreover, the complete reverse of the cartonnage is missing (compare with the two mummies with gold mask in the middle of the gallery).[426]

(e) Découpures here means the rectangular holes in the cartonnage.

(f) I agree with what is said about the spelling of the name. I here stuck to the translitteration of the signs in their syllabic values: Tt.hr or

424 The reference is to the annotated copy of the sale's catalogue in the RMO Archives (no. 3.1/3), on the fly-leaf. Likewise on the fly-leaf of a second copy, Archive 3.1/4. However, Leemans's remark is certainly not 'very true', as explained *supra* in n. 52.

425 These red lines (brackets rather than straight dashes) occur only as annotations on p. 35 of the copy 3.1/3 (see *supra*, Fig. 9).

426 This remark must refer to the contemporary display of the Egyptian department in Leiden, for which we have no precise floor-plans. Thus it may refer to any of the cartonnage mummy-sheaths of the RMO.

[Page 2]

T'.h. signifies something like *talk-face*, or *talking head*,[427] and certainly not daughter of the moon, *takerheb stealer* or *catcher of the ibis*.[428] The name of king Totôs Teôs occurs in the quarry of Mokattam 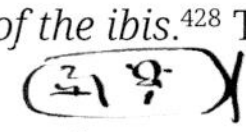, see Lauth Aeg. Chron. 1877, p. 221. Birch, Ancient history from the monuments. Egypt 1877 or 78, p. 191. Pierret Vocabulaire.[429] I do not have the Egyptian histories by Maspero and Brugsch[430] for checking this, and my annotations regarding this monarch have not yet been organized.

(g) What has been said about the date is certainly relevant. Those mummies with gold masks in the centre of the gallery are probably of the same period. However, a similar mummy is attributed to the XXVIth dynasty by Birch, no. 27 of the Archaeological Journal (1851).[431] I have an offprint of that article. A study of the family of Tsahos, which includes the large sarcophagus in the Louvre[432] and various items in Boulac, will perhaps, or most probably, decide the issue in favour of the opinion that our mummy belongs to the Ptolemaic Period. In case of an official report

[page 3]

this position which I have taken again, will have to be changed. It will please me to revise *the present* report for that occasion.

Leiden, September 15 1878 [signed] W. Pleyte

---

427 In fact, the name *Ḏd-Ḥr* has to be interpreted as 'Horus has said: ["He shall live", or similar]'. Cf. Ranke 1935, I, 411.17.

428 For this name, see Ranke 1935, I, 371.12 and II, 397. The name has not been properly explained, although the element *hb* indeed means 'ibis'; see *Wb* II, 487.1–4. Cf. also Thirion 1985, 138 (with a question mark after the element *kr*); Lüddeckens 2000, I.3, 1152–1153 (*Tꜣ-kr-hb, Tꜣ-gl-hb*). I thank Koen Donker van Heel for these references.

429 See Lauth 1877, 221; Birch 1875, 191–192 (where indeed the Mokattam inscription is mentioned); Pierret 1875, 729.

430 Doubtless referring to Maspero 1878 and Brugsch 1877.

431 I am unable to trace this reference.

432 In fact, there are two sarcophagi of priests called Djedhor in the Louvre (nos. D 8 and D 9; see *supra*, n. 423), but there is no connection with the Leiden mummy.

List of illustrations

Fig. 1. Anubis embalming Djedhor's body. Detail of Djedhor's Book of the Dead papyrus (RMO, inv. AL 61 vel 15).

Fig. 2. Caspar Reuvens, the first director of the Leiden Museum (1818–1835). Undated portrait by Louis Moritz (Collection Leiden University).

Fig. 3. The Theatrum Anatomicum in 1712. Wellcome Library (inv. 20254i).

Fig. 4. Conrad Leemans, the second director of the Leiden Museum (1839–1891). Undated photograph (Archives RMO).

Fig. 5. Willem Pleyte, the third director of the Leiden Museum (1891–1903). Undated photograph (Archives RMO).

Fig. 6. The Ghent mummy in its coffin, also containing a cat mummy. Lithograph by Kierdorff (Archives RMO).

Fig. 7. Remains of the painted and embroidered bandages of the large mummy, plus a cartonnage panel taken from the third mummy (RMO, inv. Ar32b and Ar 34a).

Fig. 8. Portrait of Jean-Baptiste de Lescluze (private collection, Belgium).

Fig. 9. Page 35 of the Lescluze sale's catalogue with the entries on the three mummies (Archives RMO 3.1/3).

Fig. 10. Page 1 of the *procès-verbal* of the 1878 autopsy (Archives RMO).

Fig. 11a–b. Coffin of Irhapiaut (RMO, inv. L.XII.2-b), lid and case.

Fig. 12. Djedhor's funeral. Detail of Djedhor's Book of the Dead papyrus (RMO, inv. AL 61 vel 1).

Fig. 13. Cartonnage of Djedhor, front (RMO, inv. L.XII.2-d).

Fig. 14. Cartonnage of Djedhor, side (RMO, inv. L.XII.2-d).

Fig. 15. Cartonnage of Djedhor, detail of upper half (RMO, inv. L.XII.2-d).

Fig. 16. Detail of triglyph-and-rosette frieze along the lateral edges of the cartonnage (RMO, inv. L.XII.2-d).

Fig. 17. Cartonnage of Hornedjitef (London, British Museum EA 6679. Image CC BY-NC-SA 4.0, © The Trustees of the British Museum).

Fig. 18. Cartonnage of Neswaiu (Stockholm, Världskulturmuseerna E.5. Photo by Ove Kaneberg, Världskulturmuseerna. By kind permission of Sofia Häggman).

Fig. 19. Garland as framed by Pleyte (RMO, inv. Am 10-b).

Fig. 20. Palm-fibre cords of garlands (RMO, inv. Am 11-c).

Fig. 21a–b. Bead net of unknown burial, with detail of chest band (Louvre N 3078, © Musée du Louvre, Dist. GrandPalais Rmn / Christian Décamps).

Fig. 22. Bandages with hieratic texts (RMO, inv. AL 51 vel 1).

Fig. 23. Bandages with hieratic texts (RMO, inv. AL 51 vel 5).

Fig. 24. Vignettes of twelve deities and a phoenix in a barque on linen (RMO, inv. AL 42–43).

Fig. 25. Fragmentary Osiris shroud (RMO, inv. AL 38).

Fig. 26. Anklet of cartonnage (RMO, inv. AL 47).

Fig. 27. Footsoles made of cartonnage, remains of string, and bandage with ink mark (RMO, inv. AL 46a–b).

Fig. 28. Sheet from the Book of the Dead papyrus (RMO, inv. AL 61 vel 6).

Fig. 29. Sheet from the Book of the Dead papyrus (RMO, inv. AL 61 vel 11).

Fig. 30. Remains of small scroll of papyrus (RMO, inv. AL 60).
Fig. 31. Amuletic necklace as restrung (RMO, inv. AL 1–35).
Fig. 32. Five vignettes on linen (RMO, inv. AL 44a–e).
Fig. 33. Six linen fragments with parts of vignettes (RMO, inv. AL 39 and 41).
Fig. 34. Six linen fragments with parts of vignettes (RMO, inv. AL 45).
Fig. 35. Linen fragments of two artificial breasts and a shroud with gilt nipples (RMO, inv. L.XII.2-l).
Fig. 36. Male mummy with female characteristics (RMO, inv. AMM 10).
Fig. 37. Linen bandage with demotic inscription (RMO, inv. AL 59).
Fig. 38. Samples of bandages (RMO, inv. AL 50).
Fig. 39. Partial shroud with figure of Isis (RMO, inv. AL 40).
Fig. 40. Two fragments of a bleached linen shroud (RMO, inv. L.XII.2-f and -k).
Fig. 41. Fragment of a red linen shroud (RMO, inv. L.XII.2-e).
Fig. 42. Fragments of fine linen (RMO, inv. L.XII.2-a).
Fig. 43. Various samples of linen (RMO, inv. AL 48): lower row from left to right cat. 166, 162, 160, 161 (left) and 167 (right), 163–164 and 165 (2x); second row cat.nos. 177, 168–170; third row cat. no. 178 (3x); upper row cat.nos. 171–175 and 176 (2x).
Fig. 44. Rolled-up bandage fragments (RMO, inv. L.XII.2-j).
Fig. 45. Rolled-up bandage (RMO, inv. AL 49-a).
Fig. 46. Four bandages (RMO, inv. L.XII.2-n).
Fig. 47. Navel (RMO, inv. L.XII.2-i).
Fig. 48. Resin (RMO, inv. AL 64).
Fig. 49. Outer coffin of Hornedjitef (London, British Museum EA 6677. Image CC BY-NC-SA 4.0, © The Trustees of the British Museum).
Fig. 50. Inner coffin of Hornedjitef (London, British Museum EA 6678. Image CC BY-NC-SA 4.0, © The Trustees of the British Museum).
Fig. 51. Hypocephalus of Hornedjitef (London, British Museum EA 8446. Image CC BY-NC-SA 4.0, © The Trustees of the British Museum).
Fig. 52. Canopic box of Djedhor (Paris, Louvre N 2644, © 2010 Musée du Louvre / Christian Décamps).
Fig. 53. Ptah-Sokar-Osiris figure of Hornedjitef (London, British Museum, EA 9736; Image CC BY-NC-SA 4.0, © The Trustees of the British Museum).
Fig. 54. Stela of Neswaiu (London, British Museum, EA 8468; Image CC BY-NC-SA 4.0, © The Trustees of the British Museum).
Fig. 55. Djedhor accompanied by the two Ma'at goddesses. Detail of Djedhor's Book of the Dead papyrus (RMO, inv. AL 61 vel 7).
Fig. 56. Canopic box of Hornedjitef (RMO, inv. AH 215).
Fig. 57. Wooden stela of Pasheryenmin (RMO, inv. AH 21 = cat. Leemans 1840, W 19).

Abbreviations

Ä & L	Ägypten und Levante
BMSAES	British Museum Studies in Ancient Egypt and Sudan
CdE	Chronique d'Égypte
EVO	Egitto e Vicino Oriente
JEA	Journal of Egyptian Archaeology
OMROL	Oudheidkundige Mededelingen uit het Rijksmuseum van Oudheden te Leiden
RdE	Revue d'Egyptologie
SAK	Studien zur altägyptischen Kultur

Bibliography

Allen, T.G., 1974: The Book of the Dead or going forth by day, Chicago.

Amenta, A./Guichard, H. (eds.), 2017: Proceedings first Vatican coffin conference, 19–22 June 2013, I–II, Vatican.

Andrews, C., 1996: Ancient Egyptian jewellery, London.

[Anonymous], 1826: Catalogue d'une collection d'antiquités égyptiennes, dont la vente se fera à Anvers, le 5 Juillet 1826, Antwerp.

[Anonymous], 1961: 5000 år egyptisk konst, Nationalmuseum, Stockholm.

Aston, D., 2000: Canopic chests from the Twenty-First Dynasty to the Ptolemaic Period, Ä & L 10, 159–177.

Athanasi, G. d', 1836: A brief account of the researches and discoveries in Upper Egypt, made under the direction of Henry Salt to which is added a detailed catalogue of Mr. Salt's collection of Egyptian antiquities and an enumeration of those articles purchased for the British Museum, London.

Aufrère, S., 1991: L'univers minéral dans la pensée égyptienne, I–II, Cairo.

Bács, T.A./Fábián, Z.I./Schreiber, G./Török, L. (eds.), 2009: Hungarian excavations in the Theban necropolis, a celebration of 20 years of fieldwork in Egypt, Budapest.

Bellion, M., 1987: Égypte ancienne, catalogue des manuscrits hiéroglyphiques et hiératiques et des dessins, sur papyrus, cuir ou tissu, publiés ou signalés, Paris.

Bierbrier, M.L., 1987: The British Museum, Hieroglyphic texts from Egyptian stelae, etc., part 11, London.

Bierbrier, M.L., 2019 (5th edition): Who was who in Egyptology, London.

Birch, S., 1855: Account of the unrolling of a mummy at Florence, belonging to the Grand Duke of Tuscany, by Professor Migliarini, with some notes and observations, Archaeologia 36.1, 161–174.

Birch, S., [1875]: Ancient history from the monuments: Egypt from the earliest times to B.C. 300, London.

Birk, R., 2020: Türöffner des Himmels, prosopographische Studien zur thebanischen Hohepriesterschaft des Ptolemäerzeit, Wiesbaden.

Bresciani, E., 1996: Il volto di Osiris, tele funerarie dipinte nell'Egitto romano, Lucca.

Brugsch, H., 1851: Sammlung demotisch-griechischer Eigennamen ägyptischer Privatleute aus Inschriften und Papyrusrollen, Berlin.

Brugsch, H., 1877: Geschichte Aegyptens unter den Pharaonen, nach den Denkmälern bearbeitet, Leipzig.

Bruschetti, P. (ed.), 1996: Il Museo dell'Accademia Etrusca di Cortona, catalogo delle collezioni, Cortona.

Bruwier, M.-C./Mekis, T., 2019: Diversity of Akhmimic funerary art in the 4th–3rd centuries BC, a case study on a priestly family, and a study on canopic chests of Akhmim in the Graeco-Roman Period, a survey in antiquities collections, in: Mosher, M. (ed.), The Book of the Dead, Saite through Ptolemaic Periods, Essays on Books of the Dead and related topics, Prescott (AZ), 3–122.

Budge, E.A.W., 1922: British Museum, A guide to the fourth, fifth and sixth Egyptian rooms, and the Coptic room, London.

Cailliaud, F., 1831: Recherches sur les arts et métiers, les usages de la vie civile et domestique des anciens peuples de l'Egypte, de la Nubie et de l'Éthiopie, suivies de détails sur les moeurs et coutumes des peuples modernes des mêmes contrées, Paris.

Caluwe, A. De, 1991: Un Livre des Morts sur bandelette de momie (Bruxelles, Musées royaux d'Art et d'Histoire E. 6179), Brussels.

Caminos, R.A., 1982: The Rendells mummy bandages, JEA 68, 145–155.

Carter, H., 1927: The tomb of Tut.ankh.amen, II, London.

Cavalier, O. (ed.), 2011: Fastueuse Égypte, Avignon.

Champollion, J.F./(Guichard, S., ed.), 2013: Notice descriptive des monuments égyptiens du Musée Charles X, Paris.

Clarke, D.L., 1978 (2nd edition): Analytical archaeology, London.

Coenen, M., 1999: The Greco-Roman mortuary papyri in the National Museum of Antiquities at Leiden, OMROL 79, 67–77.

Cooney, K.M., 2007: The cost of death: the social and economic value of Ancient Egyptian funerary art in the Ramesside Period, Leiden.

Corcoran, L.H., 1995: Portrait mummies from Roman Egypt (I–IV centuries A.D.) with a catalog of portrait mummies in Egyptian museums, Chicago.

Dawson, W.R./Gray, P.H.K., 1968: Catalogue of Egyptian antiquities in the British Museum, I: mummies and human remains, London.

Dawson, J./Strudwick, H. (eds.), 2016: Death on the Nile, uncovering the afterlife of Ancient Egypt, Cambridge.

Dodson, A./Hilton, D., 2004: The complete royal families of Ancient Egypt, Cairo.

Donadoni-Roveri, A.M., 1988: Civilisation des Egyptiens, les croyances religieuses, Milan/Turin.

Drioton, E., 1949: Encyclopédie photographique de l'art / The photographic Encyclopaedia of Art: le Musée du Louvre, Paris.

Elias, J./Mekis, T., 2019: An exemplary burial in Ptolemaic Thebes, in: Mosher, M. (ed.), The Book of the Dead, Saite through Ptolemaic Periods, Essays on Books of the Dead and related topics, Prescott (AZ), 123–169.

Fabretti, A./Rossi, F./Lanzone, R.V., 1882: Regio museo di Torino, antichità egizie, Turin.

Filer, J.M., 1999: The mummy of Hornedjitef, further information on the mummification techniques used in preparing his body, in: Leahy, A./Tait, J. (eds.), Studies in Ancient Egypt in honour of H.S. Smith, London, 97–101.

Foissy-Aufrère, M.-P./Aufrère, S./Loury, C., 1985: Egypte & Provence, Avignon.

Germer, R., 1985: Flora des pharaonischen Ägypten, Mainz am Rhein.

Giovetti, P./Picchi, D., 2015: Egitto splendore millenario, la collezione di Leiden a Bologna, Bologna.

Gray, P.H.K., 1966: Radiological aspects of the mummies of ancient Egyptians in the Rijksmuseum van Oudheden, OMROL 47, 1–30.

Gray, P.H.K., 1972: Notes concerning the position of arms and hands of mummies with a view to possible dating of the specimen, JEA 58, 200–204.

Greco, C./Oeters, V./Raven, M.J., 2012: Tuinen van de farao's, planten en bloemen van het Oude Egypte uit de collecties van het Rijksmuseum van Oudheden, Leiden.

Greco, C. (ed.), 2015: Museo Egizio, Turin.

Grimm, G., 1974: Die römischen Mumienmasken aus Ägypten, Wiesbaden.

Guidotti, M.C., 2001: Le mummie del Museo Egizio di Firenze, Florence.

Guidotti, M.C., 2003: A proposito del sarcofago tolemaico della defunta Takerheb, in: Bonacasa, N./Donadoni Roveri, A.M./ Minà, P. (eds.), Faraoni come dei – Tolomei come faraoni, Palermo/Turin, 23–26.

Guidotti, M.C., 2009: Il corredo della defunta Takerheb nel Museo Egizio di Firenze, Aegyptus 89, 21–25.

Halbertsma, R.B., 2003: Scholars, travellers and trade: the pioneer years of the National Museum of Antiquities in Leiden, 1818–1840, London.

Hasselbach, H.A., 1987: Bibliografie van W. Pleyte, OMROL 67, 93–99.

Hellinckx, B., 2002 [unpublished thesis]: Mummy equipment, bodily parts and the divine world, a study of Egyptian funerary symbolism, Leuven.

Hoeij, M. van, 1998: Nswj, a priest in Thebes, preliminary report, Medelhavsmuseet Bulletin 31, 22–45.

Hölbl, G., 2001: A history of Ptolemaic Egypt, London/New York.

Hooft, Ph.P.M. van 't/Raven, M.J./Rooij, E.H.C. van/Vogelsang-Eastwood, G.M., 1994: Pharaonic and early medieval Egyptian textiles, Leiden.

Ikram, S./Dodson, A., 1998: The mummy in Ancient Egypt, equipping the dead for eternity, London.

Jonckheere, F., 1942: Autour de l'autopsie d'une momie, le scribe royal Boutehamon, Brussels.

Kákosy, L., 1989: Dzsehutimesz sírja Thébában, Budapest.

Kákosy, L., *et al.*, 2004: The mortuary monument of Djehutymes (TT 32), Budapest.

Keimer, L./(Germer, R., ed.), 1984: Die Gartenpflanzen im alten Ägypten, II, Mainz am Rhein.

Keurs, P. ter/Wirtz, W., 2018 (eds.): Rijksmuseum van Oudheden, een geschiedenis van 200 jaar, Leiden/Zwolle.

Kockelmann, H., 2008: Untersuchungen zu den späten Totenbuch-handschriften auf Mumienbinden, Wiesbaden.

Laurent-Täckholm, V., 1940: A mummy coffin in the Egyptian Museum, Stockholm, and its plant remains, Svensk botanisk tidskrift 34, 141–161.

Lauth, J., 1877: Aegyptische Chronologie basirt auf die vollständige Reihe der Epochen seit Bytes-Menes bis Hadrian-Antonin durch drei volle Sothisperioden = 4380 Jahre, Strasburg.

Leemans, C., *et al.*, 1839–1905: Monumens égyptiens du Musée d'Antiquités des Pays-Bas à Leide, Leiden.

Leemans, C., 1840: Description raisonnée des monumens égyptiens du Musée d'Antiquités des Pays-Bas, à Leide, Leiden.

Leemans, C., 1879: Rijksmuseum van Oudheden, in: Verslagen omtrent 's Rijks verzamelingen van geschiedenis en kunst, I, 1878, The Hague, 43–66.

Leitz, C., 2002: Lexikon der Ägyptischen Götter und Götterbezeichnungen, Leuven/Paris/Dudley.

Lieblein, J., 1868: Katalog öfver egyptiska fornlemningar, I: National-Museum, Stockholm.

Lüddeckens, E., *et al.*, 2000: Demotisches Namenbuch, Wiesbaden.

Lüscher, B., 1998: Untersuchungen zu Totenbuch Spruch 151, Wiesbaden.

Manley, P./Dodson, A., 2010: Life everlasting, National Museums Scotland, collection of Ancient Egyptian coffins, Edinburgh.

Mariette, A., 1864: Notice des principaux monuments exposés dans les galeries provisoires du Musée d'antiquités égyptiennes de S.A. le Vice-Roi à Boulak, Paris.

Marshall, A./Lichtenberg, R., 2013: Les momies égyptiennes, la quête millénaire d'une technique, Paris.

Maspero, G., 1878 (3rd edition): Histoire ancienne des peuples de l'Orient, Paris.

McClintock, J./Strong, J., 1870: Cyclopedia of biblical, theological and ecclesiastical literature, New York.

Mekis, T., 2011: L'équipement funéraire de la prêtresse thébaine Nestaneteretten, CdE 86, 41–81.

Mekis, T., 2012: The cartonnage of Nestanetjeretten (Louvre AF 12859; MG E 1082) and its enigma, BIFAO 112, 243–273.

Mekis, T., 2019: Some reflections on the funerary equipment of Paiuhor, in: Mosher, M. (ed.), The Book of the Dead, Saite through Ptolemaic Periods, Essays on Books of the Dead and related topics, Prescott (AZ), 257–298.

Mekis, T., 2020: The hypocephalus, an ancient Egyptian funerary amulet, Oxford.

Meulenaere, H. De/Limme, L./Quaegebeur, J., 1985: Indices et addenda to P. Munro, Die spätägyptischen Totenstelen, Brussels.

Meulenaere, H. De, 1998: Premiers et seconds prophètes d'Amon au début de l'époque ptolémaïque, in: Clarysse, W./Schoors, A./Willems, H. (eds.), Egyptian religion, the last thousand years, studies dedicated to the memory of Jan Quaegebeur, Leuven, 1117–1130.

Miatello, L., 2008: The hypocephalus of Takerheb in Firenze and the scheme of the solar cycle, SAK 37, 277–287.

Mosher, M., Jr., 2010: An intriguing Theban Book of the Dead tradition in the Late Period, BMSAES 15, 123–172 (see http://www.britishmuseum.org/research/online_journals/bmsaes/issue_15/mosher.aspx).

Mosher, M., Jr., 2019: The Book of the Dead of Paiuhor, in: Mosher, M. (ed.), The Book of the Dead, Saite through Ptolemaic Periods, Essays on Books of the Dead and related topics, Prescott (AZ), 331–386.

Mosher, M., 2023: Illustrations in Saite through Ptolemaic Books of the Dead, in: Lucarelli, R./Stadler, M.A. (eds.), The Oxford handbook of the Egyptian Book of the Dead, Oxford, 445–484.

Munro, P., 1973: Die spätägyptischen Totenstelen, Glückstadt.

Niwiński, A., 1998: Some unusual amulets found on the Late Period mummies in Warsaw and Cracow, in: Clarysse, W./Schoors, A./Willems, H. (eds.), Egyptian religion, the last thousand years, studies dedicated to the memory of Jan Quaegebeur, Leuven, I.178–190.

Parlasca, K., 1966: Mumienporträts und verwandte Denkmäler, Wiesbaden.

Peremans, W./ Dack, E. Van 't, 1907–1986: Prosopographia Ptolemaica, Leuven.

Petrie, W.M.F., 1914: Amulets, London.

Pierret, P., 1875: Vocabulaire hiéroglyphique comprenant les mots de la langue, les noms géographiques, divins, royaux et historiques, classés alphabétiquement, Paris.

Pleyte, W., 1876: De Egyptische lotus, Nederlandsch Kruidkundig Archief, 2e bijlage tot de 29e jaarsvergadering der Nederlansche Botanische Vereeniging, 108–115.

Pleyte, W., 1882: Bloemen en planten uit Oud-Egypte in het museum te Leiden, Nederlandsch Kruidkundig Archief, 2e bijlage tot de 35e jaarsvergadering der Nederlandsche Botanische Vereeniging, 43–55.

Pleyte, W., 1884: La couronne de la justification, in: Travaux de la 6e sesssion du Congrès international des Orientalistes à Leide, II, Leiden.

Pleyte, W., 1886: Bloemen en planten uit Oud-Egypte in het Museum te Leiden, in: Nederlands Kruidkundig Archief, Ser. II vol. 4, Nijmegen, 44–55.

Quaegebeur, J., 1995: À la recherché du haut clergé thébain à l'époque gréco-romaine, in: Vleeming, S.P. (ed.), Hundred-gated Thebes, Leiden/New York/Cologne, 139–161.

Quirke, S. 1999: Two Books of the Dead of a Ptolemaic Psamtek, OMROL 79, 37–66.

Ranke, H. 1935-1959: Die ägyptischen Personennamen, I–III, Glückstadt.

Rannou, E., 1999: Rennes, Musée des Beaux-Arts, Collections égyptiennes, époque pharaonique, Rennes.

Raven, M.J., 1978–1979: Papyrus-sheaths and Ptah-Sokar-Osiris statues, OMROL 59–60, 251–296.

Raven, M.J., 1980: The 30th Dynasty Nespamedu family, OMROL 61, 19–31.

Raven, M.J., 1984: Wax in Egyptian magic and symbolism, OMROL 64, 7–47.

Raven, M.J., 1984–1985: Een 'Aegyptische Momie' uit de collectie Willem Bentinck, OMROL 65, 9–17.

Raven, M.J., 1992: Numbering systems in the Egyptian department of the Rijksmuseum van Oudheden at Leiden, OMROL 72, 7–14.

Raven, M.J., 1993: Mummies onder het mes, Amsterdam.

Raven, M.J./Taconis, W.K., 2005: Egyptian mummies, radiological atlas of the collections in the National Museum of Antiquities at Leiden, Turnhout.

Raven, M.J., 2018: The most prominent Dutchman in Egypt: Jan Herman Insinger and the Egyptian collection in Leiden, Leiden.

Raven, M.J., 2024: Single-sheet cartonnage mummy cases from elite Ptolemaic burials, in: Strudwick, N./Aston, D.A. (eds.), From objects to histories, Studies in honour of John H. Taylor, Wallasey, 477–487.

Recklinghausen, D. von, *et al.* (eds.), 2007: Ägyptische Mumien, Unsterblichkeit im Land der Pharaonen, Stuttgart.

Reuvens, C.J.C./Sandifort, G./Breda, J.G.S. Van, 1824: Voorlopig verslag van de opening van eene Egyptische mumie gedaan te Leyden, Algemeene Konst- en Letterbode, 27 Augustus 1824, 131–137.

Reuvens, C.J.C., 1830: Lettres à M. Letronne sur les papyrus bilingues et grecs et quelques autres monumens gréco-égyptiens du Musée d'Antiquités de l'Université de Leide, Leiden.

Rhind, A.H., 2002 (reprint): Thebes, its tombs and their tenants, Piscataway.

Rosati, G., 2003: Le bende iscritte di Takerheb, in: Bonacasa, N./ Donadoni Roveri, A.M./Minà, P. (eds.), Faraoni come dei – Tolomei come faraoni, Palermo/Turin, 44–49.

Rosati, G., 2009: Il Libro dei Morti di Takerheb ritrovato, Aegyptus 89, 9–19.

Rosati, G., 2013: Novità su Takerheb, in: Betrò, M./Miniaci, G. (eds.), Talking along the Nile: Ippolito Rosellini, travellers and scholars of the 19th century in Egypt, Pisa, 215–221.

Schmidt, V., 1919: Sarkofager, Mumiekister, og Mumiehylstre i det gamle Aegypten, Typologisk Atlas, Copenhagen.

Schreiber, G., 2006: Ptolemaic cartonnages from Thebes, in: Győry, H. (ed.), Aegyptus et Pannonia III: acta symposii anno 2004, Budapest, 227–247.

Schreiber, G., 2007: The final acts of embalming, an archaeological note on some rare objects in Theban elite burials of the early Ptolemaic Period, in: Endreffy, K./András, G. (eds.), Proceedings of the Fourth Central European Conference of Young Egyptologists, Budapest, 337–356.

Silvano, F., 1980: Le reticelle funerarie nell'Antico Egitto: proposte di interpretazione, EVO 3, 83–97.

Strudwick, N./Taylor, J.H. (eds.), 2003: The Theban necropolis: past, present and future, London.

Strudwick, N., 2006: The British Museum, masterpieces of Ancient Egypt, London.

Taylor, J.H., 2001: Death & the afterlife in Ancient Egypt, London.

Thirion, M., 1985: Notes d'onomastique, contribution à une révision de Ranke *PN*, RdE 36, 125–143.

Töpfer, S., 2017: The instructions of the 'Embalming Ritual' in the light of archaeological evidence, in: Kóthay, K.A. (ed.), Burial and mortuary practices in Late Period and Graeco-Roman Egypt, Budapest, 23–34.

Wagner, M., 2024: Das Grab des Ibi, Theben Nr. 36, Band II: Die beiden Sarkophage des Ibi und die Sargkammer des Psammetik, Wiesbaden.

Walker, S./Bierbrier, M., 1997: Ancient faces, mummy portraits from Roman Egypt, London.

Walle, B. Van de, 1959: Jean-Baptiste De Lescluze, négociant et armateur brugeois (1780–1858), Annales de la Société d'Emulation de Bruges 96, 64–88.

Walle, B. Van de, 1960: Jean-Baptiste De Lescluze, négociant et armateur brugeois (1780–1858), Annales de la Société d'Emulation de Bruges 97, 154–236.

Wijngaarden, W.D. van, 1932: Beschrijving van de Egyptische verzameling in het Rijksmuseum van Oudheden, deel XIV: De monumenten van het Nieuwe Rijk en van den Saïtischen tijd, Grafborden en papyruskokers, The Hague.

Wildung, D., 1977: Imhotep und Amenhotep, Gottwerdung im alten Ägypten, Munich/Berlin.

Indices

1. Deities

Amun 22, 32, 49, 85, 103–104, 107, 111
Amun-Re 48–49, 104, 110, 115
Anubis 9, 32, 85, 93, 95
Atum 76
Bastet 16
Hapy 76
Horakhte 49
Horus 31, 46, 95
Imhotep 69, 115
Isis 26, 31–33, 35, 46, 69, 77, 79, 85, 90, 93, 95
Khonsu 39, 103, 107, 111
Ma'at 85, 93, 99
Montu 49, 104
Mut 104
Nekhbet 32–33, 103, 111
Nephthys 26, 31–35, 46, 71, 85, 90, 93, 95
Nut 46
Osiris 31–33, 43, 46, 48–49, 59–60, 74, 77, 85, 88, 90, 95, 112
Ptah 115
Ptah-Sokar-Osiris 7, 89–90, 93–95, 105, 109–110, 114
Re 32, 69, 84, 88
Sokaris 26, 59, 70, 85, 92
Sokaris-Osiris 31
Sons of Horus 46, 69, 90, 93
Thoth 31, 46, 69, 85
Wadjet 32–33, 103
Wepwawet 31, 48

2. Royal persons

Akhenaten 76
Alexander 53
Apries 104
Arsinoe II 102, 114
Berenike II 102
Djedhor 101, 114, 118
Hatshepsut 107
Osorkon I 19
Philotera 114
Psamtik II 33, 39, 101, 104, 114
Ptolemy II 114
Ptolemy III 102
Ptolemy VIII 39
Tutankhamun 53

3. Egyptian personal names

Aapehty 49, 104, 114
Ankhefenkhonsu 49, 109
Ankhhor 13, 51, 53
Butehamon 76
Djedhor (others) 101, 104, 114–115, 118
Djedmonthefankh 19
Djehutir(di)s 49
Djehutymes 109–110
Harwa 26
Herankh 68
Heresankh 114
Hor 49
Hordjehuty 49
Horemheb 49–50, 61, 69, 87–88, 104, 107
Hornedjitef 49–50, 61, 66, 68–70, 87–88, 90–95, 102, 104, 107–109
Iahmes 49
Ibi 107
Imhotep 49
Irhapiaut 26–27, 89
Irthoreru 26
Khonsuemma'a[kheru] 22
Nakht 107, 109
Nebetdenehyt 49, 104, 114
Nebwenenef 109
Neferibre 26, 32–33, 39, 65, 92–93, 101, 104, 112, 114
Neferrenpet 115
Nehemsyrattawy 48, 68, 90, 92, 95, 109
Nekhthorheb 49
Nesmin 49, 104, 110

Nestanetjeretten 48–49, 68, 90, 92, 95, 102, 104, 109
Neswaiu 49–50, 54–55, 69, 87, 90, 95–96, 101–102, 104, 109
Padiamunnebnesuttawy 49
Padiheka 115
Padimenekh 115
Paiuhor 49, 68, 90, 92–93, 95, 102, 104, 109
Panesy 22
Pashery... 49
Pasheryenmin 101, 114, 116
Pasheryheby 48
Pawerem 48
Pesdet 49
Psamtik 39, 68
Sensaos 114
Taditneferhotep 49
Takerheb 26, 31–32, 36, 39, 49–50, 59, 61, 65–66, 68–70, 77, 85, 90, 92–93, 101–102, 104, 109–110, 114, 118
Tarepyt 48, 54–55, 70, 87
Tashery 49
Tasherytaapehty 49
Tasheryt(en)taihet 115
Taukesh 49
Taykhybiat 49
Tjaimu 49, 104
Wahibre 104

4. Modern names

Anastasi, D' 13, 19, 39, 76, 101, 107, 109–110
Ascherson 51, 53
Athanasi, D' 107
Barthou 21, 110, 112
Beeftingh, Van 13
Birch 85, 88, 101, 104, 114, 118
Blumenbach 15
Breda, Van 12, 15, 52
Brugsch 114
Cailliaud 55
Carnarvon 110
Champollion 13, 113
Cimba 13
Clot-Bey 13, 19
Courbarien 109, 112
Dawson 50, 87
Drovetti 109–110
Durand 110
Eberstein, Von 49
Eyben 17
Ferdinando III 109, 112
Fisher 109
Gray 15, 50, 87
Hadley 15
Humbert 13
Insinger 13–14
Jonckheere 76
Karl XIV Johan 109
Klasens 13
König 15
Lebolo 109
Leemans 13–14, 21, 26, 29–30, 33, 45, 51, 59, 101, 104, 113–115, 117
Lescluze, De 12–13, 20–25, 30, 39, 43, 52, 101, 107, 110, 112–113, 117
Maspero 13
Migliarini 50, 57, 60–61, 66, 69, 77, 85–87, 104, 114
Napoleon 11–12, 21
Piccinini 107, 109
Pleyte 7, 13–14, 17, 19, 25–26, 29–30, 43, 45–46, 48, 50–53, 55, 57, 59–61, 65, 69–71, 77, 84–87, 93, 101, 111, 117–118
Pointeau 49
Reuvens 9–13, 15, 17, 21–26, 30, 32–34, 51–52, 59, 113, 117
Rhind 109
Röntgen 15, 19
Rosellini 50
Rottiers 13
Salt 13, 55–56, 107, 109–110
Sandifort 12, 15, 52
Schneider 13
Schoor 19
Stuers, De 13
Wijngaarden, Van 13
Wilkinson 109
Willem I 11

5. Places

Akhmim 13, 92
Alexandria 13, 21, 109–110, 112
El-Hibeh 55
Karnak 49, 76, 103–104, 110–112
Luxor 109
Memphis 39, 68, 92, 114
Mokattam 118
Thebes 7, 13, 25, 39, 48, 51, 53, 55–56, 59, 66, 88, 92, 95, 101–105, 107, 110–112
- El-Assasif 107, 109–110
- Deir el-Bahari 107, 110
- Dra Abu 'n-Naga 109–110, 112
- El-Khokha 110, 112
- Sheikh Abd el-Qurneh 107, 109
- TT 32 49, 59–60, 85, 109–110
- TT 36 49, 107
- TT 52 107
- TT 83 109
- TT 157 49, 109
- TT 161 109
- TT 305–307 109
- TT 373 49

6. Periods

New Kingdom 53, 95
Ramesside Period 50
Third Intermediate Period 19, 22, 45, 49, 55, 76
Late Period 26, 39, 49–51, 53, 55, 59, 63, 101–102, 107, 114, 118
Ptolemaic Period 7, 25, 39, 48, 50, 53–55, 60–61, 63, 66, 68, 76–77, 84–88, 92–95, 101–105, 109–112, 114–115, 118
Roman Period 14, 51, 53, 60–61, 75–77, 84–85, 102

7. Museum collections

Avignon, Musée Calvet
- A 67A 48, 90, 109

Brussels, Musées Royaux d'Art et d'Histoire
- E 5288 76

Cairo, Egyptian Museum
- JE 25813 48
- JE 37017 104
- TR 21/11/16/13 48, 54–55, 70, 87

Christchurch (N-Z), Canterbury Museum 59, 85
- EA 1988.73–76 66

Cortona, Accademia Etrusca 48

Cracow, Archaeological Museum
- AS/2438 84

Derby, Derby Museum and Art Gallery
- 1872.1 49

Florence, Museo Archeologico
- 5703A 90, 109, 112
- 5703B 49–50, 57, 59–61, 66, 69–71, 77, 85–88, 90, 101, 104, 109, 112, 114
- 5704 90, 92
- 5705–5706 61
- 5715–5719 61

Leiden, Rijksmuseum van Oudheden
- AdS 1 13
- AES 14 13
- AH 21 39, 101, 114, 116
- AH 215 90, 93, 107–108
- AL 1–35 44, 69–70
- AL 36 69
- AL 37 44
- AL 38 44, 59–60, 85
- AL 39 44, 71, 73
- AL 40 44, 77, 79, 85
- AL 41 44, 71, 73
- AL 42 44, 59
- AL 43 44, 59–60
- AL 44 44, 71–72, 85
- AL 45 44, 74, 85
- AL 46 44, 61–62
- AL 47 44, 61–62
- AL 48 44, 77, 82
- AL 49 44, 77, 83–84
- AL 50 44, 77–78
- AL 51–58 57
- AL 51 44, 57–58, 74, 77
- AL 59 44, 77–78
- AL 60 44, 68
- AL 61 9, 41, 44, 65–67, 99
- AL 63 44, 70
- AL 64 44, 84
- Am 1–18 52
- Am 10-b 44, 52
- Am 11–13 52
- Am 11-c 44, 52–53
- AMM 1–27 13
- AMM 8 114
- AMM 9 84
- AMM 10-e 76
- AMM 18 19
- AMM 24-a 51, 76, 84
- AMM 25-b 76, 84
- AMS 19 39
- AMS 47a 104
- AMS 53 39
- Ar 32 12, 17–19
- Ar 34 12, 18–19
- Ar 35 12
- Ar 36 12, 19
- BA 216–218 13
- CB 1–11 13
- CB 3 19
- CI 254 13
- CI 255 13
- CI 259–260 13
- CI 281 13
- CI 335 13
- F 93/1.22 13
- F 96/5.1 13
- F 1902/5.10 13
- F 1910/5.1–2 13
- F 1942/6.1 14
- F 1948/12.2 14
- F 1954/11.2 14
- F 1956/10.1–7 14
- F 1960/1.1 14
- F 1973/9.53 14
- F 1975/11.3–4 14
- F 1980/1.12 14
- F 1982/12.7–14 14
- F 1985/3.1 14
- F 1986/3.1 14
- F 1998/11.2–3 14
- F 2004/12.2 14
- F 2010/8.2 14
- L 1 12, 15–17
- L 2 12, 15–17
- L.XII.1 13, 22–23

- L.XII.2 13, 22–25, 43
- L.XII.2-a 44, 77, 80
- L.XII.2-b 26–27
- L.XII.2-c 44, 70
- L.XII.2-d 26, 44–48, 90, 111
- L.XII.2-e 44, 77, 81
- L.XII.2-f 44, 77, 80
- L.XII.2-g 44, 52
- L.XII.2-i 44, 84
- L.XII.2-j 44, 83–84
- L.XII.2-k 44, 77, 80
- L.XII.2-l 44, 75
- L.XII.2-m 44, 75
- L.XII.2-n 83–84
- L.XII.2-o 44, 84
- L.XII.3 13, 22–23
- L.XII.4–7 13
- RO.III 13, 51

Leipzig, Grassi Museum
- 1906.429 49

London, British Museum
- EA 6677 90–91
- EA 6678 90–91
- EA 6679 49–50, 61, 69–70, 87–88, 90
- EA 6680 49–50, 61, 69, 87–88, 104, 107
- EA 6704 76
- EA 8446 90, 92
- EA 8468 90, 95–96, 109
- EA 9736 90, 94–95
- EA 9737 90, 95, 109
- EA 10037 66
- EA 20745 55

Melbourne, National Gallery of Victoria
- D 144-1982 26

Munich, Staatliche Bibliothek
- pHier. 1, 4.a–b 68

New York, Pierpont Morgan Library
- pAmherst 35 66

Paisley, Paisley Museum
- EG 203, 212, 239 49, 90

Paris, Louvre
- AF 708 90, 93, 110–111
- AF 12859 49, 90, 109
- D 8 115, 118
- D 9 115, 118
- N 2514 B 90, 95
- N 2627 85
- N 2644 90, 92–93, 110–111
- N 3078 55–56, 90, 110–111
- N 3128 104
- N 3149 68, 109
- N 3192a 68
- N 3204B 68, 109
- N 3508 E 90, 95, 109
- N 3510 E 90, 95, 109
- N 3520 A 90, 95
- N 3520 B 90, 95, 109

Philadelphia, Pennsylvanian Museum of Archaeology
- 29.86.436 90, 92, 109

Rennes, Musée des Beaux-Arts
- 873.5.6 49

Stockholm, Världskulturmuseerna
- A.04.H.04 54
- E.5 49–50, 55, 69, 87, 90, 109
- E.6 90, 109
- E.7 90, 109

St. Petersburg, Hermitage
- 822 90, 93

Turin, Museo Egizio
- C. 1569 90, 95
- C. 1599 90, 95, 109
- C. 2257 49, 110
- C. 2258 49, 110
- C. 2321 90, 92
- C. 2324 90, 92, 109
- S. 5226/1a–b 26
- S. 5229/a–b 26

Vatican, Museo Gregoriano Egizio
- 25007 26
- 38609 68, 109

Warsaw, National Museum
- 236805 49